THE BIG 50

BOSTON BRUINS

The Men and Moments That Made the Boston Bruins

Fluto Shinzawa

TRIUMPH
BOOKS

Library of Congress Cataloging-in-Publication Data

Names: Shinzawa, Fluto, 1977– author.
Title: The big 50 Boston Bruins : the men and moments that made the Boston
 Bruins / Fluto Shinzawa.
Other titles: Big fifty Boston Bruins
Description: Chicago, Illinois : Triumph Books LLC, [2016]
Identifiers: LCCN 2016033969 | ISBN 9781629372556
Subjects: LCSH: Boston Bruins (Hockey team)—History. | Hockey teams—
United States—History.
Classification: LCC GV848.B6 S54 2016 | DDC 796.96209744/61—dc23 LC
record available at https://lccn.loc.gov/2016033969

This book is available in quantity at special discounts for your group or organization. For further information, contact:

Triumph Books LLC
814 North Franklin Street
Chicago, Illinois 60610
(312) 337-0747
www.triumphbooks.com

Printed in U.S.A.
ISBN: 978-1-62937-255-6

Design by Andy Hansen
Photos courtesy of AP Images

To Elizabeth, my favorite reader

[Contents]

[Foreword]

I'm from a family of athletes. My grandfather George played baseball for Connie Mack with the Philadelphia A's. My great-uncle Charlie broke a bunch of records playing football at Harvard.

Neither George nor Charlie watched the Big Bad Bruins.

At our home in Melrose, north of Boston, we had our routine. Every game night, we'd turn on Channel 38. During intermission, my brothers and I would play mini hockey on our knees with souvenir sticks and a plastic golf ball. When we heard Fred Cusick's and Johnny Peirson's voices return, we'd sit back down and watch the game.

I was eight years old and 10 years old, respectively, when the Bruins won the Stanley Cup in 1970 and 1972. All those guys were my heroes, not just Bobby and Espo. I loved them all—Bucyk and Sanderson and Don Awrey and Dallas Smith and Gary Doak. When they won, it made me want to be a hockey player. It made me want to be an NHL player. It made me want to be a Bruin.

By my senior year at Melrose High, I finished third in scoring in the Middlesex League. I chose the University of New Hampshire without ever visiting campus because it had a Division I hockey program.

I made the team as a freshman walk-on in 1979. But I didn't play for the first two months. In December, Charlie Holt put me in for my first game against Air Force. We won 9–3. I scored seven points. That summer, Philadelphia used the last pick to draft me. I was a late bloomer coming out of high school. Maybe I'd be the same out of college.

I turned pro after my junior season. I spent most of my first professional year playing for Tom McVie with the Maine Mariners of the AHL. In March, Philly called me up. My first NHL game was at the Spectrum. My second was at Boston Garden. We were fighting against the Bruins for first place overall. I was on a line with Bobby Clarke and Bill Barber.

My parents didn't have money. My dad was a firefighter, plus he held down two other jobs. There were seven kids, so buying tickets to the Garden wasn't an option. But Dad was there for that Flyers-Bruins game. It took a lot for him to be there, but it meant a lot for him to be there, too. So as great as that first game was, that second game in Boston—against the Bruins, with my family there—was pretty awesome. I could never have played another game in the NHL, and that would have been OK. As it turns out, I went on to play almost 400 more NHL games.

Life in the NHL isn't always like that first experience. In 1988, I was playing for New Jersey. The Devils left me exposed in the waiver draft. That hurt. The year before, we made it to the conference final and I'd been a big part of that success. So being let go was a surprise. But a day later, the Bruins claimed me. I was going to play for my hometown team!

In 1990, we had a real good team. Ray Bourque was probably at his peak. Cam Neely was a menace. But I played in only 43 games because of myositis in my leg. Mike Milbury had me watch video and sit in on meetings, because it looked like my career was over. By the time we got to the Stanley Cup Final against Edmonton, I hadn't played since January. We lost in triple overtime in Game 1. We didn't recover in Game 2. By Game 3, when we got to Edmonton, my equipment was hanging in the room. Mike said, "We need an emotional lift. I want you to play tonight." I'll never forget that.

Now I make my living covering the Bruins. When people compliment me, I tell them it's what I know. I couldn't tell you the first thing about physics. But I can tell you a lot about hockey. When I'm watching, it never moves too fast for me to fully assess everything that's happening or is about to happen. I see in real time what others can only see when the tape goes in slow motion.

I dreamed of being what those guys were in the '70s. I got to the league and I played for the Bruins. It's a short list of people in the world who've experienced something they dreamed about as a kid. That's pretty cool.

—Andy Brickley

1

NUMBER FOUR

Not many of the inhabitants of Treasure Island Gardens in London, Ontario, grasped the significance of what took place on September 23, 1966. That night, the Bruins played the Maple Leafs in the first game of the preseason, which is not usually a moment of significance.

But that night, in a 1–1 tie, an 18-year-old defenseman assisted on the Bruins' only goal. The following day, after the Bruins had gathered at their hotel in Detroit for an upcoming game, Harry Sinden ran into legendary *Hockey Night in Canada* broadcaster Foster Hewitt, who had attended the Bruins-Leafs game.

"The kid's not bad," Sinden recalled Hewitt telling him. "But I think he needs some time in the minors."

"Well, maybe," Sinden replied kindly.

It goes without saying that Sinden did not heed Hewitt's advice and suggest to his bosses that Bobby Orr was not ready for the NHL. By then, even before the puck had dropped on the regular season—the first of 10 Orr would spend in Boston—Sinden, general manager Hap Emms, assistant GM Milt Schmidt, and every player in the organization

Bobby Orr won the Sports Illustrated *1970 Sportsman of the Year* award, one of many awards he would acquire throughout his career.

knew what kind of asset they had in the kid from Parry Sound, Ontario.

"It was easy to get their help, because they could see in Orr what I could see and we all could see," Sinden said of the rookie's teammates. "You, as a player, could really thrive playing with this guy. He was the greatest give-and-go player who ever played. He'd make a pass, come out from behind his own net, make a pass up to his winger, then break and get it back. He'd end up shooting on their goal from there. That's how I brought him into the team. That's the star he was. I was relying on the players to understand what a great asset they had. They did. None of them disputed it."

Orr's fate, after all, had been dictated six years earlier. While playing at a bantam tournament in Gananoque, Ontario, the prodigy's skating, smarts, and skills were so advanced that Wren Blair, a Bruins scout, identified Orr as a future franchise player. He was 12 years old. Because of Blair's insistence, the Bruins sponsored minor hockey in Parry Sound, believing the show of goodwill would pay dividends if Orr committed his services to Black and Gold.

That was no guarantee. The 1960s were the heyday of the Maple Leafs and Canadiens. Both teams landed the top amateurs. Toronto got the best players from Ontario. Montreal had a stranglehold on the French-Canadians. It left the Bruins to pick at the leftovers. It showed in their record.

Orr, therefore, was the Bruins' best chance at revival. Blair knew it. Partly because of Blair's persistence, Orr signed with the Bruins in 1962 as a 14 year old. Orr and his family liked Blair, but they also saw an opportunity in Boston for the defenseman to play right away for a rebuilding franchise instead of paying his dues for the league's behemoths. The offer to stucco the Orr family home, provide for a new car, and pay for the teenager's new suit didn't hurt either.

By locking up Orr, Blair played the biggest role in initiating the turnaround.

"Montreal and Toronto had complete control of player supply. You got what was left over," Sinden said. "That's why the guy [who] signed Orr in the battle with Toronto over him deserves the real credit for getting him here: Wren Blair. It was very hard to compete with Toronto and Montreal."

By the time Orr arrived in Oshawa to play junior hockey, there was little doubt about what was in his future. By 1966, his third and final season in Oshawa, Orr helped the Generals advance to the Memorial Cup. A groin injury slowed Orr. But he was still better than everybody on the ice.

"He was sensational then, even though he shouldn't have been playing," Sinden said. "He could shoot better than anybody else. His skating was a struggle because he was hurt with the bad groin. But he was very, very impressive."

That summer, Orr signed his first NHL contract aboard the *Barbara Lynn*, Emms' boat. Orr scored 13 goals and 28 assists in 61 games as a rookie. The Bruins went 17–43–10 and finished in last place. Orr won the Calder Trophy as the league's best rookie, and he finished third in Norris Trophy voting to Harry Howell and Pierre Pilote as the NHL's top all-around defenseman.

For the next eight years, the Norris became Orr's birthright. Even in 1967–68, when knee, shoulder, and clavicle injuries limited him to 46 games, Orr's brilliance (11–20–31) was such that voters had no choice but to classify him as the top defensive dog. By 1969-70, Orr (33–87–120) was entering the peak of his magnificence.

That year, Orr showed the league how deadly his skating had become. He was a free-flowing tsunami of prowess, turning would-be defenders into helpless bystanders. Traditional defensemen kept pucks out of their net by leaning on opponents,

FROM FRIEND TO ENEMY

In 1966, aboard the *Barbara Lynn*, Bobby Orr signed a ground-breaking contract. Fittingly, Alan Eagleson was also on board to oversee the transaction. Eagleson had approached Orr when he was a 16-year-old up-and-comer in Parry Sound, Ontario. Orr trusted Eagleson to handle his business affairs. For the first part of Orr's career, Eagleson did his job well.

Eagleson grew into one of the sport's most powerful individuals. He became executive director of the NHLPA. He was in charge of Team Canada's entry in the 1972 Summit Series. He was elected to the Hockey Hall of Fame in 1989. The same year, he was named to the Order of Canada. Without Orr, none of this would have happened.

Orr didn't know until it was too late that Eagleson was a fraud. Among Eagleson's misdemeanors was his failure to inform Orr that Jeremy Jacobs was offering his client an ownership share to stay with the Bruins. Orr left Boston for Chicago, a departure that benefited nobody except Eagleson. By the time of his retirement, Orr was near bankruptcy because of unpaid taxes. Eagleson's actions included embezzling player pension funds.

Following an investigation by *Lawrence Eagle-Tribune* writer Russ Conway, Eagleson was charged with fraud by both the FBI and Royal Canadian Mounted Police. Eagleson pleaded guilty and was given an 18-month prison sentence. He was forced to resign from the Hall of Fame and was stripped of his Order of Canada.

"There was a time after his betrayal when, had I found himself in a room alone with Alan Eagleson, I don't know what I would have done," Orr wrote in *Orr: My Story*. "He caused my entire family a lot of pain, and the anger I experienced over that ate at me for a very long time. Those feelings have now passed."

cracking them in the back in the danger areas, and strong-arming them to prevent chances. Orr revolutionized the craft of defending. Other teams couldn't score because the puck was always on Orr's stick. In the attacking zone, if Orr's shots didn't go in, Phil Esposito was regularly in place to tuck home the garbage.

Even on the penalty kill, Orr's mind was on attacking. During one game against Oakland, Orr lost a glove while shorthanded.

"He went around by the blue line, came back, picked up his glove—still had the puck," Esposito told *Sports Illustrated*. "Gerry Cheevers was on the bench, and I'm standing there and hear Cheese say to me, 'Espo, you want the Racing Form?' I said, 'Might as well; I'm not touching the puck!' Bobby killed about a minute and 10, 20 seconds of that penalty—and then he scored. Greatest thing I ever saw."

In the playoffs, the Bruins took care of the mighty Rangers in six games. They had completed the hardest part of the job. They swept the Blackhawks in four games. In the Finals, Blues coach Scotty Bowman deployed Jimmy Roberts to serve as Orr's shadow. It didn't matter. Forty seconds into overtime of Game 4, Orr scored the winning goal to end the series and give the Bruins their first Stanley Cup in 29 years. Naturally, Orr won the Conn Smythe Trophy as playoff MVP.

"Orr was the difference," Sinden said. "When we got Esposito, now we had a real scorer, the best scorer in the league. Then with Cheevers, we had three up the middle and had center ice covered."

Orr was even better in 1970–71. In 78 games, Orr scored 37 goals and 102 assists for 139 points. Orr's assist and point totals remain the NHL standard for defensemen in one season. But Orr and the Bruins, who had become the first team to win 50-plus games in one year (57), thudded into Ken Dryden and the Canadiens in the playoffs.

Orr reset and steered the Bruins back to the Cup in 1972, their second in three seasons. He went 37–80–117 in 76 games, by then, a standard output of sublimity. The Bruins took care of Toronto in five games to open the playoffs. They swept the Blues in the semifinals. It took them six games to beat the Rangers and hoist the Cup once more. Orr and the Bruins had reached their zenith.

Under normal circumstances, Orr's wizardry could have led the Bruins to more than two championships. But the NHL's expansion in 1972, in concert with the launch of the World Hockey Association, helped to pick apart a roster that could have remained stable for years. Meanwhile, Orr's knees continued to deteriorate. By 1975–76, Orr played in just 10 games for the Bruins. It would be his final season in Black and Gold. Following a contract dispute with the Bruins, Orr heeded the advice of agent Alan Eagleson—the two would part years later—and signed with Chicago.

Orr played just 26 games for his new team. Perhaps it was fate. From the start, the Bruins were the only team worthy of Orr's association.

2

THE BIG BAD BRUINS

The club that busted a 29-year dry spell, then lifted the Stanley Cup a second time two seasons later, was not just a hockey team. The Bruins of 1970 and 1972 were a cultural phenomenon that not only set the standard for how the game was played, but did so with a flair that helped turn them into icons.

The team was loaded with star power—Bobby Orr, Phil Esposito, Wayne Cashman, John McKenzie, Johnny Bucyk, Derek Sanderson, and Gerry Cheevers being its standard-bearers. To the masses, they were more familiar as Bobby, Espo, Cash, Pie, Chief, Turk, and Cheesy, as important and well known in their days as Pelé, Sting, and Oprah, other one-named iconic personalities.

"The city was in a Bruins fog," said Mike Milbury, a schoolboy star at Walpole High School when his hometown team won the Cup in 1970. "It's hard to describe. People—family and friends— would gather on a Thursday night to watch the game. The next day, that was the discussion. There was always something to discuss. They were one of the great entertaining teams of all time. If it wasn't Orr, it was Espo. There'd be a fight with Cashman, or Pie McKenzie

doing something crazy. Cultlike is the best way to describe it. People were consumed with the Bruins."

They turned hockey into something the NHL had never seen. Before the Bruins strutted their way through the Rangers, Blackhawks, and Blues, nobody played defense like Orr. There still hasn't been a defenseman to match No. 4's singular approach. Cashman turned puck battles in the corners into armed conflicts. Esposito and Bucyk claimed ownership on the net-front area to punch in goals—the ones goalies were fortunate to stop Orr from scoring.

Yet it was the long, dark prelude to the light of 1970 that turned the first Cup run into magic. The Bruins had not been good for a long time. For six seasons in the 1960s, the Bruins made last place their birthright. In Boston, hockey had become irrelevant.

"They had been in the cellar through the '60s," said Harry Sinden. "The year before I came, they finally got to fifth place. When I got there, I took them back to sixth. They ended up making a great move when they made the trade for Esposito and [Ken] Hodge and [Fred] Stanfield. We got size back. But the first team I had here was not a good team. That's the way they'd been playing for 5–6 years."

The Big Bad Bruins woke the city from its slumber. They stormed through the regular season, going 40–17–19. Orr lit up the league for 120 points. Their reward: a first-round showdown against the powerful Rangers. The team on Broadway was loaded, from Ed Giacomin in goal to Brad Park on defense to Jean Ratelle and Rod Gilbert up front. The teams were closely matched. The difference was Orr.

After a six-game battle with the Rangers, the Bruins had little time to catch their breath before staring down the Blackhawks. Stan Mikita, Bobby Hull, and Tony Esposito would make any opponent shiver in fear. Not the Bruins. After four straight wins over Chicago, the Bruins were set for a final against St. Louis, an expansion team that had entered the league just three years earlier. The Bruins' heavy lifting was over. The Blues simply didn't have enough good players to hang with the Bruins' stars.

"We had a better team than they did," Sinden said. "Their defense could not handle guys like Bucyk, McKenzie, and Esposito. Scotty Bowman was their coach. So what they did, in typical Bowman fashion, he took Jimmy Roberts and put him on Orr. As we broke out of our own end, he would stay with Orr. No matter where Orr went, he'd be with him. What it did was it ended up that Bucyk became the star."

The Bruins won the Cup in the most fitting fashion possible: in overtime, in style, and off Orr's stick. As Orr flew through the air following his championship goal, the defenseman knew he

FROZEN IN TIME

It is the most iconic photograph in NHL history. Bobby Orr, having scored the game-winning goal in overtime in Game 4 of the 1970 Stanley Cup Final, is in full flight, courtesy of Noel Picard's stick. Orr, the Bruins, and the NHL have Ray Lussier to thank. Lussier was a photographer for the *Boston Record American* working at Boston Garden that day. When another photographer vacated his spot along the glass, Lussier saw his opening and took advantage of the opportunity. In 2010, the Bruins immortalized the moment Lussier captured by unveiling a statue of an in-flight Orr in front of TD Garden.

A close second would be the picture snapped by Montreal photographer Roger St. Jean following Game 7 of the semifinal between the Bruins and Canadiens in 1952. It captures Bruins goalie Jim Henry, eyes black because of a broken nose, bowing slightly to greet a bloodied Maurice Richard in the postgame handshake line.

had brought hockey back to Boston for good. During the Cup celebration at Boston's City Hall Plaza, McKenzie poured beer over Mayor Kevin White's head. This was the way the Bruins operated.

The Big Bad Bruins were even bigger and badder in 1970–71. They had the misfortune, however, of running into their fiercest rivals. But even the hated Habs needed something more than their usual skill and luck to topple the mighty Bruins that season. They played their ace: Ken Dryden, the law school student turned puck-stopping prodigy. A dynastic run came to an end, with Dryden playing the hero.

The beaten Bruins did not allow the upset to linger. They roared right back into the postseason in 1972. They took care of Toronto in five games in the opening round. In the second round, for the second time in three seasons, they swept the Blues. This set them up for another showdown against the Rangers. Familiar combatants such as Park, Ratelle, Gilbert, Giacomin, Vic Hadfield, and Walt Tkaczuk pushed back against the Bruins to stretch the series to six games. But the Bruins blanked the Rangers 3–0 in Game 6 to win their second Cup in three years. Again, Orr scored the winning goal, while Cheevers turned back all 33 shots.

Had it been business as usual in the NHL, the Bruins could have chased several more Cups, despite Orr's creaking knees. But in 1972, the NHL expanded by two teams, while the World Hockey Association came to life. All of a sudden, the star-studded roster had been diminished following the loss of Ed Westfall to the expansion Islanders and the WHA's recruitment of Cheevers, Sanderson, McKenzie, and Ted Green. The Bruins couldn't recover from the one-two punch.

"The team was not going to stay together," Sinden said. "It had to be rebuilt."

The end of the run was as difficult for the city to comprehend as it was to embrace its beginning. Thirty-nine years would pass until the Cup returned to Boston. But the Big Bad Bruins made hockey meaningful in Boston once more. Kids who might have preferred other sports couldn't wait to get to the rink because of the Bruins' influence. The 1970 and 1972 Bruins made hockey cool again.

3

THE BRILLIANCE OF BOURQUE

Ray Bourque could not help but be nervous. In the fall of 1979, after the Bruins made him the eighth overall pick of that year's draft, Bourque attended his first pro training camp. He was 18 years old, lining up alongside legends such as Brad Park, Wayne Cashman, Jean Ratelle, Gerry Cheevers, and Gilles Gilbert. As such, Bourque was not a lock to make a team that had finished atop the Adams Division the year before and lost to Montreal, the eventual Stanley Cup champs, in the semifinal.

But Bourque had a calmness to his game that was mature beyond his years. Regardless of the competition he was about to face, Bourque believed he was good enough not just to make the Bruins as a teenager, but do well as an NHL rookie.

"I've got to tell you that I was very confident of my ability to play in the NHL," Bourque said. "I think you really need that to do well, have success, and be the best you can be—to really have confidence in yourself."

Bourque sailed through camp and made the final roster. The No. 29 he was given at the start of camp became No. 7, a number he wore until 1987. On October 11, 1979,

Bourque made his NHL debut against Winnipeg. With his father and stepmother in attendance at Boston Garden, Bourque scored a goal and an assist.

The points would continue for the entire season. By the end, Bourque had racked up 17 goals and 48 assists in 80 games. In the playoffs, Bourque added two goals and nine assists in 10 games. New records, both within the organization and the league, became a regular occurrence for the rookie. He set a team high in assists for a rookie. His 65 points were good enough to set an NHL record for the highest total by a rookie defenseman. He became the first non-goalie in league history to win the Calder Trophy as the NHL's top rookie and to be named a First Team All-Star in the same season.

"It was fantastic. I loved it," Bourque said of his rookie experience. "I really believed in myself and thought I could play in that league. From Day 1 when I got to camp, things went really well for me."

The Bruins could thank a trade from the previous season for the pick that resulted in Bourque. On October 9, 1978, the Bruins traded Ron Grahame to Los Angeles for the Kings' first-round pick in 1979. The Bruins were deep in goal with Cheevers and Gilbert. They could afford to let Grahame go for a future first-rounder.

By August 9, 1979, the day of the draft, the Bruins were in the market for defense. Park, 31 years old, was ready to hand off leadership of the blue line. Bourque didn't project to be as flashy as Park. But the Bruins drafted Bourque, thinking he would become a steady, robust, and dependable defenseman. It didn't take the Bruins long to figure out that Bourque's future was even shinier than they expected.

The kid from Montreal, who admired the play of Larry Robinson, Serge Savard, and Guy Lapointe, was not as graceful as Park. He was not as wondrous as Bobby Orr. But Bourque continued the

ALL IN THE FAMILY

On January 19, 2013, Chris Bourque made history. The son of Ray Bourque made his Bruins debut in a 3–1 win over the Rangers. The player who had grown up in the dressing room at TD Garden had made a dream come true by working the same real estate his father once dominated.

"It was awesome," Bourque said of his first Bruins game. "I've been here in the crowd to watch these games, but to play in front of this crowd was a special moment for me."

The Bourques are one of five father-son combinations to play for the Bruins. The others: Harvey and Bill Bennett; Albert G. and Albert T. DeMarco; Ron and John Grahame; and Ken R. and Ken D. Hodge. It's possible a sixth could join them. Ryan Donato, son of ex-Bruin Ted Donato, was one of the team's second-round picks in 2015.

legacy of the Bruins' stranglehold on dressing the best defenseman in the league, a chain that would endure when the team signed Zdeno Chara in 2006.

The quality that endeared Bourque to his coaches (Fred Creighton, Harry Sinden, Butch Goring, Terry O'Reilly, Mike Milbury, Rick Bowness, Brian Sutter, Steve Kasper, and Pat Burns) was his reliability. Every coach knew he could depend on Bourque to shut down top-line opponents, even wizards such as Wayne Gretzky and Mario Lemieux, help lead the offense, and play 25–30 minutes every game.

Bourque's level of play was always high and never wavered, regardless of the opponent or time of season. Even when other forwards did their best to pound the sand out of Bourque, the defenseman responded by standing up to the punishment, retrieving pucks, and moving them the other way. On defense, Bourque was like a redwood: strong, sturdy, and impossible to dislodge. Once Bourque started to go on the attack, his skating took him through center ice and put him in good position after gaining the offensive zone. When he crossed the offensive blue line, Bourque took advantage of his vision, creativity, and heavy shot to put pucks behind goalies or snap them onto teammates' sticks.

Bourque made all of his teammates better. By Bourque's count, he played 757 games with Don Sweeney, his usual stay-at-home partner. Like Bourque, Sweeney cruised past the 1,000-game threshold, partly because of how he played alongside his longtime teammate. Bourque's game also complemented the crash-and-bang style of Cam Neely. When Bourque got the puck up the ice, it usually landed on Neely's stick.

"If your best player is the hardest worker, you've got a chance, as a team, to do something special," said former teammate Andy Brickley. "That's what he was all about."

In 1985, the 24-year-old Bourque became the club's captain. He would wear the "C" for the Bruins through 2000, becoming the longest-tenured captain with one team in NHL history. It took until 1987, when he scored 23 goals and 72 assists in 78 games, for voters to recognize Bourque as the league's best all-around defenseman. It was the first of five Norris Trophies he would win.

The following year, Bourque advanced to the Stanley Cup Final for the first time. Although the Bruins lost to the Oilers, Bourque had the satisfaction of beating the Canadiens in the playoffs that year. It was the first time the Bruins had beaten the Canadiens in the playoffs in 45 years. Two years later, the Bruins were back in the final against the Oilers. Once again, the Bruins fell short. It was the closest Bourque would come to a Cup until he was traded to Colorado.

Bourque's fitness was world class. It allowed him to log heavy minutes and stay healthy throughout his career. In 2000–01, his 22nd and final season in the league, a 40-year-old Bourque still scored seven goals and 52 assists in 80 games for the Avalanche. Bourque left the game at the top after he won the Cup that had eluded him for his first 21 seasons.

Bourque concluded his career with 1,612 games. He scored 1,579 points, the most of any defenseman in league history. He was named a First Team All-Star 12 times. He is the pace setter for multiple Bruins records: most games (1,518), goals by a defenseman (395), points (1,506), and assists (1,111).

Upon reflection, Bourque credited his attitude of getting better every day as the reason behind his consistency. He was never satisfied with just being good. He wanted to be great.

"When the best players are the best people, everybody has to follow," Bourque said. "I learned that early as a Bruin. What being a Bruin was all about was working hard, setting the example, and doing it the right way. I couldn't have dreamed of having that kind of career. I never stopped to really think about what I was doing when I was doing it. Once it was done, I'd look back and go, 'Wow.' It was incredible. I had a lot of fun. I played with great guys, great teammates, and great friends."

4

THE MOST INTENSE RIVALRY IN SPORTS

On April 10, 2008, Tim Thomas made his NHL playoff debut. The Bruins lost to the Canadiens at Bell Centre that night 4–1. Until then, Thomas did not comprehend the significance of the moment.

Playoffs. Bruins-Canadiens. In Montreal.

"I felt like a Roman gladiator," Thomas said of stepping out of the dressing room and onto hostile ice.

Before Thomas hit the Bell Centre ice in the playoffs, he did not understand the heat of the Bruins-Canadiens rivalry. Once he did, the goalie finally realized what it meant to participate in the most intense rivalry in sports.

Through 2016, the Bruins and Canadiens had squared off 733 times in regular season history, the most head-to-head games of any two teams in the league. They have done battle in 34 postseason series and 177 games, also the most in NHL history. They have played each other nine times in Game 7, the most in any North American major professional sport. There are generations of players on both sides who have bled, cried, and battled their way through such games to the

degree where just the sight of the logos—the Spoked B on one end, the CH on the other—causes the blood to boil.

"I've talked to a lot of guys who have played for Montreal, guys who are my friends, guys that I respect," said Andy Brickley. "I agree with them that Montreal, they do it right. I respect everything on how they run their organization and how they treat their past players, guys who have meant a lot to their organization. But I still hate them. I do."

THE RICHARD RIOT

On March 13, 1955, an incident between two hockey players—playing for the Bruins and Canadiens, naturally—mushroomed into a cultural event that landed in textbooks of Canadian history.

During a Boston-Montreal game at Boston Garden, Bruins defenseman Hal Laycoe clashed with Canadiens legend Maurice Richard. The Rocket took exception to the tangle. Richard went after Laycoe multiple times, including with his stick. When linesman Cliff Thompson tried to break up the fight, Richard punched the official.

Three days later, NHL president Clarence Campbell suspended Richard for the remainder of the regular season and the entire postseason. Canadiens fans were outraged. Some of them interpreted the punishment as an Anglophone coming down hard on a French-Canadian.

On March 17, Campbell attended the Red Wings–Canadiens game at Montreal Forum. Demonstrators gathered at the rink before the game. Shortly after Campbell arrived, somebody threw a can of tear gas inside the arena. The game was forfeited to Detroit and the Forum was evacuated. The Richard Riot, as it came to be known, continued outside the rink. The violence spread to St. Catherine Street, one of the city's main drags. The riot resulted in over $100,000 in property damage and more than 100 arrests.

The Bruins and Canadiens launched their NHL existences on equal footing. In 1929, after sweeping the Canadiens in three straight, the Bruins won their first of six Cups. By 1943, the franchises had met in the playoffs four times. Each won twice.

That was the end of any sniff the Bruins would get of postseason success against the Canadiens. From 1945 until 1988, the Canadiens grabbed all 18 playoff meetings in every way possible, from bad fortune to jinxes to roster domination, thanks to their Quebec inroads on the province's top amateur players.

"I have a lot of respect for Montreal. A lot of respect," said Harry Sinden. "They were kind of like how the St. Louis Cardinals are to baseball. They had all the advantages in the world. All the advantages. They controlled the draft. They had the pick of the French-Canadians. Imagine having your pick of guys like that. They had some fantastic players and fantastic teams. I did have respect for them. A lot."

Some of the players, teams, and stories belong in legends more than record books. Hal Laycoe versus Maurice Richard. The Big Bad Bruins versus Les Glorieux. The 1971 juggernaut versus Ken Dryden, the unknown rookie dubbed a giraffe by Phil Esposito. Too many men versus Guy Lafleur and Yvon Lambert. Brad Marchand versus P.K. Subban.

The rivalry was such that even New England Patriots owner Robert Kraft recalled its ferocity when growing up in Massachusetts.

"I remember as a young boy, being under the covers of my bed late at night with my transistor radio under the pillows, listening to the likes of Milt Schmidt and Sugar Jim Henry against Boom Boom Geoffrion and Rocket Richard," Kraft said upon the unveiling of the 2016 Winter Classic at Gillette Stadium. "Listening to those games and then having these two teams come here, it's a great thrill."

The rivalry wasn't just about one team vs. another. It meant far more. It was about the Bruins' blue-collar style versus the Canadiens' freewheeling artistry. It was about American pride against Francophone heritage. The hatred seethed to the point where even fellow Canadians in Atlantic Canada became Bruins fans because of their dismissal of everything that had to do with the Canadiens.

"Going into that barn was something special," Mike Milbury said of playing in Montreal Forum, "with how into it those people were. Everybody was on top of each other. When you walked the streets, people would approach with, 'Mil-beh-ree, we'll get you tonight,' in those French accents. They'd heckle you on the street. It was a special event. The people made you feel like it was a special event. You'd be that much more prepared to be ready for that event."

It was because of the one-sided nature of the rivalry that the 1988 playoff win for the Bruins was something that still brings smiles to the victors' faces. A 45-year curse was finally dead. They had slain the mythical dragon that had tormented earlier generations for 18 consecutive playoff series.

The 1988 win did nothing to diminish the rivalry. If anything, it made it even fiercer. In 2002, the Bruins were favored to roll over the Canadiens in the first round of the playoffs. But a Kyle McLaren forearm shiver to Richard Zednik sparked an emotional Montreal rally. In 2004, with future Boston coach Claude Julien behind the Montreal bench, the Canadiens shook off a 3–1 series deficit to win three straight games and send the Bruins empty-handed into the lockout. Four years later, with Julien in Boston, the underdog Bruins took the favored Canadiens to the edge before losing in Game 7. In 2011, the Bruins topped the Canadiens in overtime of Game 7 in the first round as the launchpad for their Cup run.

In 2014, the rivalry reached a flashpoint when Shawn Thornton sprayed Subban during play with a water bottle, then Milan Lucic threatened Dale Weise in the handshake line at the conclusion of the series.

"Good rivalry," Thornton deadpanned before the 2014 clash. "Both teams get into it. So I'm going to enjoy it."

5

BACK
TO THE
TOP

or a day, during one of the most heated playoff series most of them had ever seen, the Bruins played the part of tourists instead of hockey players. They strolled up and down Main Street next to Mirror Lake in civilian clothes, not the suits they were always required to wear. They had earned a day off.

The Bruins were in Lake Placid, New York, the home of miracles. They had pulled off one of their own the night before: entering Montreal's Bell Centre, the most hostile rink in the league, to grab a 4–2 win in the opening round of the 2011 playoffs. The down-and-out Bruins, losers of the first two games at home, were back in the fight. But with two idle days before Game 4 in Montreal, the Bruins decided to decamp in the village made iconic by a group of fellow scrappers 31 years earlier.

That the Bruins' march to the Stanley Cup included a pit stop in Lake Placid was the stuff of movies. The Bruins were backstopped by Conn Smythe Trophy winner Tim Thomas, the American everyman whose primary goal in becoming a hockey player was to appear in the Olympics. The Bruins had their doubters after Zdeno Chara missed Game 2

of the opening round because of an illness, Patrice Bergeron was unavailable for the first two games of the Eastern Conference Final because of a concussion, and Aaron Rome knocked out Nathan Horton in Game 3 of the Stanley Cup Final. The Bruins had to overcome 0–2 series deficits against Montreal and Vancouver.

But like the 1980 Americans, the Bruins believed in the unbelievable. Regardless of the roadblocks set in their way, the Bruins barreled through them with confidence and attitude. Consider the Game 4 come-from-behind 5–4 overtime win against the Canadiens. The Bruins, down 3–1 in the second period, launched their rally when Andrew Ference fired a puck past Carey Price, then flipped off the Montreal crowd. Ference's gesture captured the spirit of the 2010–11 Bruins: feisty, aggressive, and never out of it.

Ference was an important player. He was physical, gritty, and reliable. When Dennis Seidenberg moved up to Chara's right side for Game 3 against the Canadiens, Ference skated on the No. 2 pairing alongside Johnny Boychuk.

But Ference's value was important off the ice, too. Sometime during the stretch run of the regular season, Ference acquired an old Bruins Starter jacket on eBay. He bought it as a gag. But it became a critical symbol for the team during their championship run.

After each win, the jacket would go to the player who had contributed most to the victory. And not necessarily with an important goal or save. The Bruins believed that little things were important to team success: checks, blocked shots, and backchecks. The players chased the jacket each game because of what it represented. It brought the team closer.

So it was especially haunting for the Bruins after their 8–1 pounding of the Canucks in Game 3. It would have been Horton's responsibility to hand off the jacket to his most deserving teammate. Horton was the jacket's steward following his winning

Andrew Ference presented retired Bruin Mark Recchi with the coveted team MVP jacket at the start of the 2011–12 season.

goal in Game 7 of the Eastern Conference Final against Tampa Bay. Horton scored the lone goal of the penalty-free game to launch the Bruins into the final.

Horton, the first-year Bruin, had never been to the playoffs before 2011. The right wing, the third overall pick in the 2003 NHL Draft, had played in 422 games for the Panthers. All of them were in the regular season. Horton was tired of losing. So at the end of 2009–10, Horton requested a trade. Florida GM Dale Tallon granted Horton his wish.

Horton settled well into life as a Bruin. He and fellow widebody Milan Lucic became the thunderous bookends on David Krejci's flanks. Despite his lack of a playoff pedigree, Horton elevated his performance in the tightest of games. In Game 5 against Montreal, Horton scored the winner in double overtime. Two games later, also in overtime, Horton's snapper beat Price to vault the Bruins into the second round against Philadelphia.

But nothing about Horton's future was certain after Rome closed on the right wing and delivered a shot to his head at 5:07 of the first period. Horton left on a stretcher and was taken to nearby Massachusetts General Hospital. He had suffered a concussion. He would not play again in the series.

Horton felt good enough, however, to make an unexpected visit to the dressing room after the Bruins' 4–0 Game 4 win and hand over the jacket to Rich Peverley, who scored two goals. Horton was also well enough to travel to Vancouver for Game 7 and pour some melted TD Garden ice onto the Rogers Arena surface before the puck dropped.

Symbolism worked well for the Bruins. But so did good, hard-nosed, thorough play. Part of the reason they dispatched the Flyers, their nemesis from the previous season, in four straight games in the second round was their in-your-face approach. They played

ON THIS DATE

FEBRUARY 18, 2011

The Bruins trade Blake Wheeler and Mark Stuart to Atlanta for Rich Peverley and Boris Valabik. It frees up enough salary for them to acquire Tomas Kaberle from Toronto later that day for Joe Colborne, a first-round pick, and a second-rounder. Kaberle arrives in Ottawa that night to play in a 4–2 win.

physical, structured, and disciplined hockey in Game 7 against the Lightning. And when everything was on the line in Game 7 against the Canucks, their toughest players accepted the challenge.

For most of the first period, the Bruins' skilled players weren't having much luck. Lucic, Krejci, and Peverley were chasing the puck. So were Bergeron, Brad Marchand, and Mark Recchi. The third line of Michael Ryder, Chris Kelly, and Tyler Seguin couldn't get any traction. Amid the Canucks' surge, the Bruins' fourth line of Daniel Paille, Gregory Campbell, and Shawn Thornton punched back.

The threesome, known as the Merlot Line because of the color of their practice jerseys, was a fourth line in name alone. Thornton, the rough-and-tumble right wing, repeatedly classified the speedy Paille and the cerebral Campbell as forwards who could be third-liners on other teams. The Bruins' depth dictated otherwise. The would-be third-liners regularly took advantage of their matchups. They blended speed, physicality, and smarts to strip opponents of pucks and create zone time and scoring chances at the other end.

The fourth line did just that against the roaring Canucks. By the time the fourth-liners' teammates found their rhythm, the Canucks had faded off their initial push. Marchand, who started the season on the fourth line, scored twice. So did Bergeron, his linemate.

Shortly after the Cup-clinching win, Chara approached commissioner Gary Bettman to claim his prize. The biggest and strongest player in the league almost fell backward when he lifted the Cup over his head. The attrition of the season had nearly worn Chara out. But he had enough gas left to skate around the Rogers Arena ice with the Cup and celebrate in the dressing room with his teammates, family members, and friends.

One last time, the Bruins presented their cherished jacket to the player who deserved it the most. There was no question of who the recipient would be. Recchi, the future Hall of Fame Player, was calling it quits. Recchi left the game on top with a Cup and the jacket. The two most powerful symbols of the season had come together under a deserving steward.

6

A DYNASTY INTERRUPTED

In one way, Ken Dryden had no business doing what he did in 1971. Here was a 23-year-old law school student, with just six games of NHL experience, stepping into the most heated rivalry in pro sports to foil a dynasty in the making. Nobody could have scripted such a scenario, not with the Big Bad Bruins chewing up the rest of the league en route to what should have been an easy repeat championship.

But in another way, Dryden was meant to step into the Montreal net and steal a Stanley Cup that was all but destined to land in Boston for a second straight year. As a collegian at Cornell, Dryden had owned Boston and its famous rink. Over three years of standout play at Cornell, Dryden went 76–4–1, earning All-America honors each season. In 1966–67, Dryden was in goal at Boston Garden for back-to-back ECAC Tournament wins over Boston College and Boston University. The following year, Dryden and the Big Red turned the same trick over BC and BU at the Garden once more. In 1968–69, Dryden strutted out of the Garden with two more ECAC Tournament wins, this time over BU and Harvard.

"I have been coming to Boston for more than twelve years, the last eight years with the Canadiens, and in sports parlance, Boston is *my* town, the Boston Garden *my* rink, the Bruins [Boston University, Boston College, Harvard] *my* team," Dryden wrote in *The Game*. "In the endless panorama of any season, it is my own personal landmark—a city, a team, a rink, a game I always look forward to; a base where, when things go badly, I find solid ground; a launch pad where, when things must go well, they always do."

Dryden was a groundbreaker in more ways than one. At 6'4", he was one of the tallest goalies to play in the NHL at the time. Like most goalies, Dryden played a stand-up style, and as such, was subject to openings simply because of his frame. But Dryden was nimble enough to scoot around his crease as quickly as most of his smaller counterparts.

Dryden was also one of the rare NHLers not fully invested in a career as a pro hockey player. He wasn't satisfied with being an Ivy League graduate. Dryden's future was in law, which required him to hit the books, regardless of his other calling as an NHL puck stopper. In 1970–71, his first pro season, Dryden attended McGill Law School while playing for the Montreal Voyageurs of the AHL. Even when he was called up to the Canadiens, Dryden continued his studies. It would have been hard enough for a normal goalie to replace Rogie Vachon at the end of the season, command control of the crease in the playoffs, and stare down Bobby Orr and the Bruins. That Dryden did so while practically doing his homework between the pipes made his performance even that much more spectacular.

Consider, after all, the might of the 1970–71 Black-and-Gold roster. The Bruins won a league-record 57 games. Phil Esposito scored 76 goals and 76 assists for 152 points, most by any NHLer. Orr recorded 102 assists, which remains the standard for NHL defensemen. A league-record four teammates scored 100-plus points: Esposito, Orr, Johnny Bucyk, and Ken Hodge. The four were named First-Team All-Stars. The lineup was the stuff of fantasy, among the best in NHL history.

A rookie turned the kings into peasants.

KIDS ARE ALL RIGHT

As a collegian, Ken Dryden turned Boston Garden into his playground. He has company. The college games that have taken place at the Garden and its successor, especially the ones involving the four Boston schools, have been just as entertaining as the NHL tilts. The competition is at its hottest during the Beanpot Tournament, the annual gathering of Boston College, Boston University, Harvard, and Northeastern.

The Bruins have plenty of alums with ties to the four Beanpot schools. Some of the most famous include Craig Janney, Brian Leetch, and Bob Sweeney (BC); Dave Silk, Mike Sullivan, and Shawn McEachern (BU); Ted Donato, Peter Chiarelli, and Don Sweeney (Harvard); and Ferny Flaman, Chris Nilan, and Dan McGillis (Northeastern).

The Bruins concluded the regular season with two meetings with Montreal in the last three games. They dismissed the Canadiens in both games 6–3 and 7–2. By then, they knew the Canadiens would be their first-round opponents. But Dryden, even though he was on the varsity roster at the time, didn't play in either game. Montreal coach Al MacNeil made the smart move of keeping Dryden out of the net both times to preserve his confidence. MacNeil knew Dryden would be his starter in the playoffs. The last thing MacNeil needed was to see the Bruins light up his young goalie in games that meant nothing.

On the other side, the Bruins didn't know who would be in the opposing goal to start the playoffs. Two years earlier, Vachon was in net when the Canadiens beat the Bruins in six games in the semifinal.

"Personally, I don't care who plays goal for them," John McKenzie told the *Boston Globe*. "But the guy has to go with Vachon. He's the big guy, the one who has the experience. He has to go the first game."

Dryden got the call. At first, it didn't look like the right one. Dryden and the Canadiens lost Game 1 to the Bruins 3–1. Through 40 minutes of Game 2, the Bruins looked like they were on cruise control, leading 5–2. But the Canadiens stormed back to score five third-period goals and take Game 2 7–5. In hindsight, Dryden believed even after the Game 1 loss that the series could be a long one.

"In my opinion, the turning point came in the dressing room right after the first game," Dryden told *Sports Illustrated*. "That was when we all seemed to realize that the Boston Bruins were just another hockey team. We talked it over and we agreed that except for Orr their team wasn't a bloody bit better than our team—that was the real turning point."

When the series returned to Montreal Forum, the Canadiens took Game 3 3–1. The Bruins rallied to take the next two games, leaving them one win short of ending Dryden's run. It never happened. Being the cerebral type, Dryden understood the pressure of the moment. He read his law books to stay calm. He would joke that reading about trusts put him right to sleep. The Canadiens routed the Bruins in Game 6 8–3. With the series tied at 3–3, Dryden finally started to get jittery. The night before Game 7, Dryden made the mistake of watching a Bruins highlight show. Dryden saw the Bruins scoring goal after goal on him.

But Dryden recovered when the game started. The Canadiens won 4–2 to end the series and finish off the Bruins. With 32 seconds remaining in regulation, Dryden finally understood what he and his teammates were about to accomplish.

"Then it happened—seven games of feelings, too busy, too afraid to feel before, were suddenly released and swept over me," Dryden wrote. "And for thirty-two seconds I got a rare and precious gift: I felt victory *while* it was happening."

7

MR. BRUIN

O n May 15, 1967, Milt Schmidt did something that changed the Bruins in one of the biggest ways in franchise history. As the Bruins' new general manager—predecessor Hap Emms had already announced his pending resignation—Schmidt made his first trade to upgrade his forwards. Out: Gilles Marotte, Pit Martin, and Jack Norris. In: Phil Esposito, Ken Hodge, and Fred Stanfield.

"I consulted with others in the organization, but these were the deals I wanted," Schmidt told the *Boston Globe*. "Losing Marotte is a hard thing, but you have to give up something to make a worthwhile trade."

It would be Schmidt's best trade and one of the sharpest ever pulled off by any executive. Esposito, Bobby Hull's setup man in Chicago, developed into an all-around threat with his new team. In Boston, Esposito wasn't just a disher anymore. He was a scorer, one who complemented Bobby Orr's back-end wizardry with his touch around the net. Hodge, Esposito's wingman, was an excellent supporting actor. Stanfield, 23 years old at the time of the trade, developed into a consistent 20-goal scorer. The three ex-Blackhawks helped

the Bruins win the Stanley Cup in 1970 and 1972, confirming the brilliance of Schmidt's transaction.

For any other executive, it would have been a career-defining move. Schmidt, however, was not just any other executive.

Schmidt is Mr. Bruin. On October 9, 1935, the 17-year-old Schmidt became Bruins property as a player. In 1950, the 32-year-old Schmidt succeeded John Crawford as team captain. On December 25, 1954, following his retirement as a player, Schmidt took over as Bruins coach from Lynn Patrick. Then when Emms declared his time as GM to be over, Schmidt was promoted. Schmidt served as GM until 1972, when the Bruins won their second Cup in three seasons.

No other individual has served as player, captain, coach, and GM for the Bruins. His name is on the Cup four times—twice as a player,

FROM THE ICE TO THE CORNER OFFICE

On May 20, 2015, Don Sweeney was named general manager. He became the fourth former Bruin to assume the position, following Hap Emms, Milt Schmidt, and Mike O'Connell. While Sweeney is the eighth GM in team history, only three others knew the feeling of pulling on a Black-and-Gold jersey and how such an experience could frame his off-ice career.

"I think one of the distinct advantages I have is that I've been a Boston Bruin," said Sweeney, the first Bruins draft pick to become GM. "I was a Boston Bruin for 15 years, knocked on the doorstep of the Stanley Cup, and then won it as part of the management group."

From the 2015–16 team, the first he managed, Sweeney was one of five ex-Bruins working in hockey operations. Sweeney's colleagues and fellow former players were president Cam Neely, director of player development Jay Pandolfo, and scouts P.J. Axelsson, Dennis Bonvie, and Dean Malkoc.

and two more times as a GM. In 1961, Schmidt was inducted into the Hockey Hall of Fame. Had the Hall waited for Schmidt to do his thing as an executive, he might have made it in the builders' category as well.

"He's always in a good mood," said Patrice Bergeron, who passed Schmidt on December 9, 2015, for 11th place on the team's all-time scoring list. "Always wants to tell stories about back in the day. He's the ultimate Bruin, really. That's what I think about when I think about him and the way he handles himself. Just a true gentleman. He's definitely a legend for the world of hockey, but also for the Bruins too. He's a true legend and a role model for everyone."

As a player, the sprightly boy from Kitchener, Ontario, grew into a sturdy 6'0", 185-pound NHL center. Schmidt served as the fulcrum of the Kraut Line, the threesome of Kitchener players with Woody Dumart and Bobby Bauer on the wings. The three childhood friends, who lived together in a Boston suburb during their time with the Bruins, became one of the league's best lines. Schmidt and the wingers won their first Cup in 1939. The 20-year-old Schmidt served as the bridge from the previous generation of Bruins greats: Eddie Shore, Dit Clapper, and Cooney Weiland.

Two years later, the Bruins turned the trick again. They fell short of the championship in 1940, the in-between season. But Schmidt and his friends pulled off a league first. Schmidt led the NHL in scoring with 22 goals and 30 assists for 52 points. Dumart (22–21–43) and Bauer (17–26–43) were right behind Schmidt, allowing the Kitchener Kids to finish 1-2-3 in league scoring, the first line in NHL history to do so. Schmidt played at an all-out pace, skating and shooting and passing and defending at a reckless tempo.

Despite his all-around prowess, Schmidt did not win the Hart Trophy as league MVP until 1950–51, when he scored 22 goals and 39 assists for 61 points as a 32-year-old. The Bruins lost to the Maple

"Mr. Bruin" Milt Schmidt, pictured here with fellow Bruins legend Bobby Orr, is the only individual who has served as player, captain, coach, and GM for the team.

Leafs in the playoffs that season, with Schmidt only able to record one assist in six games. That he even played, according to team physician Tom Kelley, was a feat.

"He's got two bad legs but a good heart," Kelley told the *Boston Globe* regarding the Game 4 status of Schmidt, who was playing on two injured knees. "Anybody else, I'd say no. But Schmidt, yes, he'll play."

Schmidt's on-ice achievements could have been even greater had he not said goodbye to the Bruins for three seasons. On February 10, 1942, Schmidt and his linemates played in their final game before reporting to the Royal Canadian Air Force. The Kraut Line left the ice on the shoulders of the Bruins and Canadiens.

"Much to their credit in spite of how tough we were playing against one another, after the game was over, both Montreal and Boston players hoisted us on their shoulders and carried us off the ice," Schmidt told the Hockey Hall of Fame. "The ovation from the crowd was fantastic. It just goes to show that you can have pretty bitter enemies out on that ice, but after the game is over, we're all friends, and I think that has a lot to say about the people who play the game."

The Kraut Line finished out the rest of the 1941–42 season in Ottawa with the RCAF team. Schmidt spent the war in England. As the joke went in Boston, that's also where the Bruins' power play went in hiding during Schmidt's absence.

While Schmidt's game eventually returned following his wartime service, his knees could not stand up to the abuse. Schmidt retired on Christmas Day 1954, then stepped behind the Bruins bench. Schmidt served as coach for 726 games, second most in team history after Art Ross (772). Schmidt did not win any Cups as a coach. But it trained his vision and team-building approach for his days as GM.

"We are interested in the development of our own young players," Schmidt told the *Boston Globe* upon his promotion. "We have some young ones on the farm clubs we certainly will protect. But there would be such a thing as going too far with youth. There must be a balance."

Schmidt was true to his word. By then, Orr had completed his first NHL season. In short order, Schmidt acquired Esposito, Hodge, and Stanfield. The dynasty was beginning to take shape.

8

ESPO SCORES
ON THE
REBOUND

Phil Esposito was angry. On September 8, 1972, Esposito and his Canadian teammates had lost to the Soviet Union in Game 4 of the Summit Series 5–3. Esposito wasn't just angry about the loss. He was peeved with the booing that accompanied it—on home ice, no less, at Vancouver's Pacific Coliseum.

So when Esposito conducted a postgame on-ice interview with CTV, the center had something to say.

"For the people across Canada, we tried. We did our best," Esposito said. "For the people that boo us, geez, all of us guys are really disheartened and we're disillusioned and we're disappointed in some of the people. We cannot believe the bad press we've gotten, the booing we've gotten in our own buildings."

By then, Esposito had the right to deliver a speech about something bigger than a lost hockey game. Esposito's remarks were about nationalism and pride and the Cold War, some of the sentiments involved in the eight-game epic pitting Canada against the Soviet Union. Earlier that year, Esposito had won his second Stanley Cup in three seasons. The player who had earned a punting out of Chicago had grown into a respected and powerful leader, one who could speak on behalf of his country.

"Every one of us guys, the 35 guys that came out and played for Team Canada, we did it because we love our country," Esposito said. "And not for any other reason. No other reason."

Eddie Shore shook his manager, Art Ross', hand as he headed back out onto the ice for the first time since injuring the Maple Leafs' Ace Bailey in an infamous incident.

This wasn't always Esposito's role. After three full seasons in Chicago, the Blackhawks saw fit to move Esposito, Ken Hodge, and Fred Stanfield to the Bruins for Gilles Marotte, Pit Martin, and Jack Norris on May 15, 1967. Chicago general manager Tommy Ivan wasn't sure Esposito would progress beyond serving as Bobby Hull's setup man. Chicago coach Billy Reay wasn't sold on Esposito. The Blackhawks' inaccurate forecast on the then-25-year-old Esposito helped turn the Bruins' fortunes around.

At the time, the Bruins were fighting for relevance. Bobby Orr had completed his rookie season. But the Bruins had finished in sixth place in 1966–67. There was not much optimism in Boston. The Esposito blockbuster helped give the Bruins hope.

In his first Black-and-Gold season, Esposito scored a career-high 84 points (35 goals, 49 assists). He was just getting started. In 1968–69, Esposito busted through a previously untouched milestone. Esposito became the first player to score at least 100 points. He didn't just reach the century mark, either. Esposito, centering Hodge and Ron Murphy, shattered the 100-point threshold with a 49–77–126 season. The center who passed first in Chicago had become a regular recipient of the puck.

"I don't care if the puck goes in off my head," Esposito told *Sports Illustrated.* "Here in Boston, though, I'm carrying the puck more. In Chicago we gave it off to the wings. And my wings here are getting me the puck from the corner. A center can't ask for anything more."

Esposito was a slam-dunk choice to win the first of his two Hart Trophies as the league MVP. It was the beginning of Esposito's heyday as the front-and-center pivot, ready to pot goals from the slot or wheel pucks to open teammates.

"The difference is that when Phil was with the Blackhawks, he had to give me the puck all the time," Hull told Stan Fischler in the latter's book *Boston Bruins: Greatest Moments and Players.* "Now, he can keep it for himself. He's gone from being the little toad in the big pond to being the big toad in the little pond that turned out to be a big pond. Boston thought that Bobby Orr would lead them out of the wilderness. But Bobby couldn't do it alone. Orr and Esposito; they complemented each other."

Esposito turned the front of the net into his office. He became so good at scoring garbage goals that a bumper sticker became popular around Boston: "Jesus saves, but Espo scores on the rebound!" The left-shot center did not need much time to flash his wrists and deposit pucks that were once on his stick into the back of the net.

In 1969–70, Esposito, Orr, and the rest of the Bruins won the Stanley Cup. They came up short the following season, but Esposito enjoyed a record-breaking year. In 78 games, Esposito scored 76 goals, a record that would stand until 1982 when Wayne Gretzky

BEST TRADES

Chicago GM Tommy Ivan did not do himself any favors when he traded Phil Esposito, Ken Hodge, and Fred Stanfield to the Bruins on May 15, 1967. Ivan lost the trade in a big way. Ivan has company when it comes to GMs losing to the Bruins.

Others include the Rangers' Emile Francis (Brad Park, Jean Ratelle, and Joe Zanussi for Esposito and Carol Vadnais); Vancouver's Jack Gordon (Cam Neely and a first-round pick for Barry Pederson); Los Angeles' Dave Taylor (Byron Dafoe and Dmitri Khristich for Sandy Moger, Jozef Stumpel, and a fourth-round pick), Toronto's John Ferguson Jr. (Tuukka Rask for Andrew Raycroft); and Tampa Bay's Brian Lawton (Mark Recchi and a second-round pick for Matt Lashoff and Martins Karsums).

blew it to pieces. Esposito ripped 550 pucks on net, which remains the league's high-water mark.

In 1971–72, Esposito scored 66 goals and 67 assists to lead the Bruins with 133 points, mostly centering Hodge and Wayne Cashman. Esposito helped the Bruins win their second Cup in three seasons. That fall, Esposito helped the Canadians rally from their 3–1 deficit to claim the Summit Series.

"He had the courage to go on TV between periods and say that the team and players didn't deserve the abuse Vancouver fans and fans across Canada were heaping on them," Don Cherry, his former coach, wrote in *Grapes: A Vintage View of Hockey*. "He said that the players were truly doing their best and that, instead of booing and ridiculing, they should all get behind the team. It's the first time a hockey player rallied a country. Phil Esposito turned around the fans, the media—and most of all, he turned around the players."

Cherry and Esposito had grown close. It was Cherry, after all, who broke the news to Esposito that he was no longer a Bruin. The Bruins were on a road trip in Vancouver when Bruins GM Harry Sinden and Rangers counterpart Emile Francis pulled the trigger on the blockbuster on November 7, 1975. First, Cherry told Esposito he had been traded. Then Cherry confirmed what Esposito feared: that New York would be his destination. The trade caught everyone by surprise, from its participants to its observers.

"I was thinking back to the time when Esposito was traded to Boston from Chicago," Canadiens coach Scotty Bowman told the *Boston Globe*. "Nobody really thought of that being so one-sided at the time. You really have to take the position that one side might know more than the other side about the individual players. There can always be more than meets the eye in looking at statistics and ages. Let's say it might be immediately better for New York, but better long range for Boston, with [Brad] Park only 27 years old."

After being traded to the Rangers, Esposito played five more seasons before retiring in 1981. Esposito's numbers are almost comical: 1,590 career points (10th most in league history), 717 goals (No. 6), 1,012 points as a Bruin (third most after Ray Bourque and Johnny Bucyk). He was named to the Hockey Hall of Fame in 1984. Few Hall of Fame elections are as easy to make.

9

THE START OF NASTY

On December 13, 1933, Boston homicide detectives were interviewing an unlikely witness. At the time, Eddie Shore was a star defenseman for the Bruins. But the hockey player was in danger of becoming charged with a serious crime. Ace Bailey, one of Shore's opponents, was in critical condition.

The night before, Shore was involved in one of the NHL's most infamous incidents. The Bruins were hosting the Maple Leafs at Boston Garden. As Shore engaged in one of his trademark rushes with the puck up the ice, he was tripped by Toronto's King Clancy. The disturbance was enough to set off the flammable Shore. After Shore got to his skates, the first Leaf he saw was Bailey. Shore approached Bailey and blasted him from behind.

The hit would end Bailey's career and nearly cost him his life. The force of the collision sent Bailey tumbling to the ice, where he hit the back of his head. Observers did not need much time to realize that Bailey was in trouble.

"Bailey was lying on the blue line, with his head turned sideways, as though his neck were broken," Frank Selke, Toronto's assistant general manager at the time, wrote

in *Behind the Cheering*. "His knees were raised, legs twitching ominously. Suddenly an awesome hush fell over the arena. Everyone realized Bailey was badly hurt. [Defenseman Red] Horner tried to straighten Bailey's head, but his neck appeared to be locked. Red skated over to Shore, saying, 'Why the hell did you do that, Eddie?'"

The Bruin, who had not identified the severity of Bailey's condition, responded in a typical Shore manner. He smiled without remorse. Horner dropped Shore to the ice with a punch. Meanwhile, Bailey was also on the deck, his skull fractured because of the fall. Upon admittance to Boston's Audubon Hospital that night, Bailey suffered a cerebral hemorrhage. He was transferred to Boston City Hospital, where Dr. Donald Munro conducted two procedures to relieve pressure in Bailey's brain. Even after the second surgery, Bailey's odds of survival were not good. The NHL suspended Shore indefinitely.

Later that month, Bailey's condition improved. Bailey would live, although he would never play hockey again. Frank Patrick, the NHL's managing director, amended Shore's suspension from indefinite to 16 games. It was a banishment that, in coach Art Ross' opinion, was too long.

"We can't win without him," said Ross, according to his authorized biography *Art Ross: The Hockey Legend Who Built the Bruins*. "Since he's been out...we have dropped in the league standings until now we're at the bottom. More than that, the team doesn't have the appeal that it has when Shore is playing. I for one am willing to admit that he is half our team. He has been out for seven home games and the receipts have fallen off more than you would believe."

The incident captured both the ferocity and the appeal of Shore's approach. From the time Shore became a Bruin in 1926–27 until his exit in 1939–40, nobody in the NHL played with the

ON THIS DATE
MARCH 21, 1933

The Bruins conclude 1932-33 with a 3–2 win over the Rangers. Eddie Shore finishes the season with eight goals and 27 assists along with 102 penalty minutes in 48 games. He becomes the first Bruin to win the Hart Trophy as league MVP.

defenseman's degree of abandon, nastiness, or drive. Shore helped the Bruins win Stanley Cups in 1929 and 1939. He was named a First Team All-Star seven times. He was elected to the Hockey Hall of Fame in 1945. Shore remains the only defenseman to win the Hart Trophy four times as league MVP.

But Shore also finished sixth in Bruins history with 1,038 penalty minutes, an indication of the level of disregard he had for both the rule book and his opposition. The rugged Saskatchewan farm boy didn't just beat other players. He beat them up.

Shore would not have become a Bruin without two circumstances. First, the Western Hockey League folded. Shore, who had been playing for the Edmonton Eskimos, was left without an employer. Second, Bruins owner Charles Adams made the wise decision to acquire Shore, known as the "Edmonton Express," and six other ex-WHLers for $50,000. It would be among Adams' sharpest investments.

When he arrived in Boston, Shore served as Bobby Orr's trailblazer. Like Orr would do in the decades to come, Shore excelled at skating up the ice while handling the puck. But while Orr twirled around helpless defenders, Shore rolled over them. As a rookie, Shore scored 12 goals, a stunning total for a defenseman in an era when blue liners were not encouraged to exit their own zone. Shore also racked up an NHL-record 130 penalty minutes. Shore's thump-first style made him a hero at home and a villain on the road. Either way, fans packed the buildings to cheer or jeer the one-of-a-kind defenseman.

In January 1929, fans in Montreal prepared to watch Shore and the Bruins take on the Maroons. They were almost disappointed. According to *Sports Illustrated*, on January 2, the Bruins' train to Montreal departed North Station without their star defenseman. Shore had missed the train because his taxi had been delayed in an accident. The next train to Montreal would not make it in time for the game. Sleet was grounding airplanes. Shore had to take a limousine to Montreal.

The limo's passenger soon turned into its driver. After the chauffeur drove the limo into a ditch, Shore took over the wheel. Even though Shore found a service station that installed chains on the tires, the drive did not go well. Snow and ice froze the wiper blade to the windshield. Shore had to remove the windshield's top half to see the road, which put his face and hands squarely in the elements' crosshairs. After another spin off the road and a visit to a ditch, Shore had to walk one mile before he found a farmhouse.

"I paid $8 for a team of horses," Shore told *Sports Illustrated*, "harnessed the horses and pulled the car out of the ditch. We weren't too far from Montreal and I thought we'd make it in time if I could keep the car on the road."

Shore arrived at Montreal's Windsor Hotel at 5:30 PM. He ate a steak dinner and took a nap. Teammate Cooney Weiland had to pour several glasses of water on Shore to rouse him for the game. Shore scored the only goal in the Bruins' 1–0 win. Naturally, he was called for two penalties. But aside from the time he spent in the penalty box, Shore played every other minute of the game. Even for a legend like Shore, the game and the ordeal chased the boundaries of a Hollywood script.

10

THE FIRST BOSS

In 1926, $300,000 was an unthinkable amount of money. Only the wealthiest of executives could consider the sum anything other than fantasy. Charles Adams qualified as one of those businessmen.

By then, Adams was rich. The native of Newport, Vermont, had become the chairman of First National Stores, considered the country's first supermarket chain. Two years earlier, Adams' wealth had allowed him to launch the Bruins for $15,000, becoming the first American franchise in the NHL.

But like most expansion franchises, the Bruins did not acclimate well to the initial rigors of the league. In 1924–25, their inaugural season, the Bruins went 6–24–0 and finished in last place. Even before the season's conclusion, it was clear the Bruins did not have enough good players.

"Building a business, no matter whether it's in sport or commercial life, is a real task. But that is what owner Charles Adams of the Boston Bruins is trying to do," John J. Hallahan wrote in the *Boston Globe* on December 23, 1924. "He has been striving to give Boston a professional hockey team that will make the fans realize that there is a vast difference between the play of the amateurs and of the professionals, and he hopes before the season is over to get together a team of players representative of this sport-loving city."

ON THIS DATE

DECEMBER 1, 1924

The Bruins play their inaugural game at Boston Arena against the Montreal Maroons. They beat Montreal 2–1. Fred Harris scores the Bruins' first-ever goal. Carson Cooper scores the winning goal.

They improved slightly in their second season of existence, going 17–15–4 and scoring a fourth-place finish. Carson Cooper, limited to only 12 games because of a knee injury in 1924–25, led the Bruins with 28 goals in 36 games. The Bruins won their final game of the season over the Maroons 1–0. But they missed the playoffs by one point because on the previous night, Pittsburgh had defeated Ottawa to secure third place.

Naturally, the boss was displeased. Lionel Hitchman and Sprague Cleghorn, the Bruins' two best players, needed help to compete with the league's more robust rosters. It fell to Art Ross, the Bruins' coach and general manager, to execute Adams' desire to field a more competitive team.

By then, the Western Hockey League's prominence was fading amid the NHL's rise. Frank Patrick, the league's president, identified its existence would not last for long. Ross and Patrick initially discussed a plan of selling some of the league's players to the Bruins. The conversations expanded significantly. Patrick wanted to do something big—selling the entire league and all of its players.

Such a transaction would give much-needed player capital not only to the Bruins but to some of its American competitors. Adams literally bought into the vision. The owner underwrote the sale of the Western Hockey League for $300,000. It was a landmark deal that transformed the NHL and gave the Bruins the star they needed. For their portion of the fee, the Bruins received seven players, including their franchise defenseman: Eddie Shore.

Adams' money allowed the deal to take place. But it was also Adams' hiring of Ross that led to the transaction. Upon a recommendation from Thomas Duggan, a sports promoter in Montreal, Adams hired Ross to serve as the franchise's vice president, coach, and general manager. Adams could not have landed a greater visionary and thinker than Ross.

HOME ICE

Boston Garden's first event in 1928 was not a hockey game, but a boxing match. The building, dreamed up by boxing promoter Tex Rickard, was designed to give fight fans an up-close view of the sweat and blood coming off the faces of the punchers. It was an appropriate design for a rink that would feature more famous fights between hockey players than between boxers. Thanks to Rickard's design, Bruins fans enjoyed seats that were practically on top of the ice to watch the players do battle.

The Bruins' first game at the Garden on November 20, 1928, was a mob scene. Charles Adams held back rush tickets to be sold that night just prior to puck drop. It helped create a frenzy for approximately 15,000 fans to storm the new building and watch the Bruins lose to the Canadiens 1–0. Sylvio Mantha scored the lone goal on Tiny Thompson.

It wasn't just the way the fans seemed like part of the ice that made it a hard place for opponents to play. The sheet was 191 feet long and 83 feet wide instead of the standard 200-by-85 NHL surface. As such, the Bruins were regularly built to take advantage of the smaller dimensions. Size, physicality, and grit complemented the rink. Bruins fans did not complain.

"If the plans to promote a professional hockey team in Boston this Winter materialize, Boston surely will have a noted man as manager of the combination in Art Ross," wrote the *Boston Globe* in an unauthored story on October 4, 1924. "He has been appointed vice president, and is one of the best-known, all-around sportsmen in Canada."

Under Ross' guidance and the new blood infused from the Western Hockey League deal, the Bruins began to improve in 1926–27. Shore, the former Edmonton Eskimo, scored 12 goals that year, his first NHL season. By 1927–28, Shore's second season, the Bruins improved to 20–13–11, finishing first in the division.

In 1928–29, the Bruins moved from Boston Arena to the brand-new Boston Garden. Adams helped bring the building to life by guaranteeing $500,000 in gate receipts through the arena's first five years of existence. The arena, designed by Tex Rickard, did not take long to give its new tenants home-ice advantage. The Bruins won their first Stanley Cup in their first season in their new home. Shore and Harry Oliver, two of the seven players the Bruins acquired in the Western Hockey League transaction, played important roles. Five years into their existence, the Bruins fulfilled the ferocity of their name.

When he bought the team, Adams was not sure what to call it, although he knew what its primary color would be. According to the *Boston Globe*, Adams' retail stores, horses, cows, pigs, and hens were all brown. At first, Adams thought the Browns would be his new team's name. Concern grew, however, over whether its fans would call them the Brownies, a name that did not strike Adams' fancy.

According to *The Bruins: Brian McFarlane's Original Six*, Bessie Moss, Ross' secretary, was most likely to have come up with the name. The Bruins made their NHL debut on December 1, 1924, at Boston Arena, defeating the Maroons 2–1.

Adams served as the organization's steward until 1936, when he transferred stock to son Weston Adams. Charles Adams died in 1947 and was inducted into the Hockey Hall of Fame in 1960. In 1974, the NHL created divisions in the Wales Conference. It was fitting that the Bruins played in the newly named Adams Division after their founder.

11

THE
PIONEER

In 1949, Art Ross was named to the Hockey Hall of Fame in the players' category. The induction was a long time coming. The talented defenseman won the Stanley Cup in 1907 with the Kenora Thistles. The following year, while with the Montreal Wanderers, Ross won the Cup a second time. Ross' contributions to hockey as a player, however, could not compare to what he would achieve off the ice.

It is no surprise that on March 3, 2016, when Claude Julien tied Ross for the most wins as a Bruins coach, he did not dare to put himself in the same category.

"The thing that comes to mind is humbling," said Julien, who broke Ross' record of 387 wins on March 7 following the Bruins' 5–4 victory over the Panthers. "It really is humbling because this guy, I've said before, is an icon. He's a legend. I don't have a trophy named after me. Those are all things where there's a big difference between Art Ross and myself. The fact that I've avoided being fired for the last nine years helps get that many wins here. I just feel fortunate, and most of all obviously humbled, by that achievement."

Julien, or any other contemporary coach, would struggle to change the game as much as Ross did in his iterations as player, coach, and general manager. The all-around athlete (football, rugby, boxing, and baseball were among his other pursuits) liked to rush

The Art Ross–designed nets make their debut in a Bruins game. The Bruins beat Chicago 3–1.

the puck, stickhandle around defenders, and pressure the net. Ross was credited with 85 career goals in 167 games.

But Ross was also conscious about playing good defense. In 1915, Ross played for the Senators of the National Hockey Association. In the playoffs, the Senators faced off against the Montreal Wanderers, one of their chief rivals. The Senators won Game 1 4–0. Ross scored one of the goals. But with home ice going back to the Wanderers for Game 2, the Senators had to make adjustments. In Game 2, the underdog Senators dropped three skaters back, including Ross, to make sure the Wanderers couldn't generate much offense. Montreal won Game 2 1–0. But the system helped the Senators claim the series 4–1 and win the NHA championship. Observers at the time weren't sure whether to credit Ross or Ottawa coach Al Smith for the approach. But it's believed the system, dubbed kitty-bar-the-door by noted Montreal Herald columnist Elmer Ferguson, was the inspiration behind later defense-first strategies such as the neutral-zone trap.

Ross' prowess as a player and thinker caught the attention of Charles Adams. When the Boston businessman launched the Bruins in 1924, Adams wanted the man he saw play for the Wanderers. Ross would be the Bruins' first GM and coach. On December 1, 1924, with Ross behind the bench, the Bruins beat the Montreal Maroons in their first game 1–0. But the roster required improvement. Ross pursued Lionel Hitchman and Sprague Cleghorn from Ottawa. They were good acquisitions. Ross would do even better.

In 1926, Ross approached longtime hockey acquaintance Frank Patrick with his concern about the Boston roster. Patrick and his brother Lester were in charge of the Western Hockey League, which was under heavy pressure from the NHL. Ross and the Patricks devised a plan about doing something bigger than just acquiring a player here and there. With Adams' financial endorsement, Ross executed the sale of the entire league, which allowed the Bruins to land Eddie Shore, their cornerstone piece. Finally, Ross had the player he needed to chase the Cup.

Shore, Ross, stingy goalie Tiny Thompson, and the Bruins won their first Cup in 1929. As valuable as Thompson was to Ross in the net, there would be one occasion where he would serve his coach best while on the bench. During Game 2 of the opening round of the playoffs against Montreal in 1931, Ross pulled Thompson for an extra attacker. The maneuver didn't work, but it caught the attention of hockey observers, who had watched the first goalie pull in the NHL.

"It was a daring move and the Bruins kept the Frenchmen hemmed in," wrote the *Montreal Gazette*, "but the gong sounded before there was any score."

Ross resigned as coach in 1934 and was replaced by Frank Patrick. It allowed Ross to focus more of his time on managing the roster. Ross made good use of his singular focus as GM when he trained his sights on Bobby Bauer and Woody Dumart, then playing for Kitchener. The teammates convinced Ross to consider Milt Schmidt as well. Landing the Kitchener Kids was one of Ross' shrewdest moves.

Ross' departure from the bench lasted only one season. Patrick, who by then had grown apart from Ross, left the organization following the 1934–35 season. Ross' return to the bench coincided with Charles Adams transferring his ownership of the Bruins to son

Weston Adams. Again, Ross' foresight with his roster served him well with the team he had to coach.

In the fall of 1937, Ross signed young goalie Frank Brimsek, projecting him to be Thompson's future replacement. Even Ross didn't think Brimsek's services would be needed so early. But at the start of 1938, an eye injury to Thompson gave Brimsek his opportunity. Even after Thompson recovered, Ross had made up his mind. On November 28, 1938, Ross wheeled Thompson, the goalie who had helped the Bruins win their first Cup, to Detroit. The move paid off. Brimsek turned into "Mr. Zero," Mel Hill became "Sudden Death" following his overtime heroics against the Rangers, and the Bruins won the Cup. According to *Art Ross: The Hockey Legend Who Built the Bruins*, the GM/coach considered that year's championship the greatest thrill of his career in Boston.

Ross had other achievements that extended beyond the Bruins. In 1927, the league adopted a net Ross had designed. Ross' net was a B-shaped creation with two circular frames. The design eliminated the previous net's uprights, which were infamous for pucks bouncing off them and out of the cage, resulting in disallowed goals. In 1929, as a member of the NHL's rules committee, Ross helped to introduce the forward pass to promote more scoring. In 1940, Ross filed a patent for a puck that would be easier for players to control. Ross' design was a puck with a distinctive and predetermined contour that would eliminate its sharp corners.

Ross' most famous contribution to hockey was his name. In 1947–48, the NHL introduced the Art Ross Trophy, awarded each season to the league's leading scorer. Ross donated the trophy to the NHL and thus had it named in his honor. Elmer Lach was the Art Ross Trophy's first winner after scoring 30 goals and 31 assists in 1947–48. A year later, Ross had the turn of accepting the honor of entering the Hall of Fame.

12

THE
TRADE

It was not Phil Esposito's fault the Bruins started 1975–76 with a 5–5–2 record. Nor was Brad Park to blame for the Rangers' 5–7–1 stumble after the puck dropped on the season. But Harry Sinden and Emile Francis, their respective general managers at the time, believed each star player would be best served playing for his competitor.

Esposito was a legend in Boston. Since his arrival from Chicago, Esposito served as the perfect up-front complement to Bobby Orr's wizardry on the back end. Esposito helped the Bruins win Cups in 1970 and 1972. During the season in between, Esposito pumped in 76 pucks, a mark that paced the league until 1982, when Wayne Gretzky set the unbreakable record of scoring 92 times.

Esposito thought he would be a Bruin for a long time. After Esposito signed an extension with the Bruins in 1974, Sinden told his center, "I can never see me trading you." Esposito interpreted Sinden's remark as a guarantee he would not be moved.

"Desperate times," Sinden said with a laugh, "call for desperate measures."

Esposito was 33 years old. The year before, he had lit

up opponents for 61 goals and 66 assists in 79 games. But Sinden didn't think Esposito's game was trending in the right direction. The Bruins needed a change that year, and so did the Rangers. Neither GM believed trade talks would escalate to the degree they did.

"We both started lousy, the Rangers and ourselves," Sinden said. "We had some kind of meeting in Buffalo, and I met Emile Francis there. I said, 'You interested in doing anything?' He said, 'Yeah.' I said, 'I don't want to do fourth-line stuff.' He felt the same way. We thought about it and met again. He said, 'What about Esposito?' To which I thought, *I didn't think he'd go quite to Esposito, but he did.* So I said, 'What about Park?' I don't think he thought I would go to Park. He said, 'I'd consider that.'"

Park was 27 years old, still in the prime of his career. The year before, Park scored 13 goals and 44 assists in 65 games. Park, the second overall pick in 1966, played a 200-foot game. He also played with an edge. He didn't like the Bruins.

The trade started to come together. Sinden dispatched scout Bart Bradley to follow Park and the Rangers. There were concerns about Park's knee. Bradley compiled viewings on Park from three games. Bradley declared Park fit to play and a good fit for the Bruins. At the time, the Bruins knew that Orr's health was tentative at best. They needed help on defense.

The Bruins wanted reinforcements up front as well as Park. They identified Jean Ratelle as their preferred center to replace Esposito. Ratelle was 35 years old and past his most productive seasons. But his cerebral approach would allow Ratelle to remain a good player despite his age.

The Bruins were on the road in Vancouver when Sinden and Francis agreed to the trade on November 7, 1975. It was up to coach Don Cherry to break the news to Esposito in the team's hotel.

"Phil, I might as well give it to you straight; there's no use beating around the bush," Cherry wrote in *Grapes: A Vintage View of Hockey*. "Phil, you've been traded."

"His body contorted," Cherry wrote. "He was in physical and mental agony. He got up, sat down; got up again, sat down again. At least five minutes went by before he even said a word; then the words came blurting out."

Esposito was angry at being traded, but especially irked by being moved to the Rangers. He did not want to go to New York. At the same time, Ratelle was not thrilled about becoming a Bruin.

"Ratelle was a star player. He didn't want to come either," Sinden said. "He was very reluctant to leave New York. But we went down and talked to his wife and agent, and he decided to come. I don't think he ever regretted it. Both Park and Ratelle appeared to be lifetime Rangers. It's one of those trades that nobody thought would work. Phil was a lifetime Bruin. For him to play for another team, people didn't think it would work. They didn't think Park would work here. Emile and I weren't sure either."

Things exploded in Boston after the news came out. Upon returning from his office to his home, Sinden encountered a television truck parked outside. Local news anchor Natalie Jacobson was waiting for Sinden on his couch. During an interview, kids threw eggs at Sinden's house.

Sinden traveled to Oakland to meet the team, which was scheduled to play the Seals on November 9. When he checked into the team's hotel, Sinden ran into Orr in the bar.

"I knew the players were upset," Sinden said. "I didn't know how they were going to treat me. Bobby helped me. He said, 'We were terrific last night. This is really going to work.'"

The Bruins finished first in the Adams Division in 1975–76. Park scored 16 goals and 37 assists in 43 games for the Bruins. He was a point-per-game player in the playoffs, as the Bruins lost to Philadelphia in the semifinal. The Rangers did not qualify for the playoffs that season or in the year after.

Esposito did not take the trade well. He held a grudge against Sinden and the Bruins.

"Phil was really disappointed in me," Sinden said. "He felt I had guaranteed that I wouldn't trade him. Remove the word guaranteed, and he had a point."

The frosty relationship melted on December 3, 1987. The Bruins retired Esposito's No. 7 in the most dramatic fashion—having Ray Bourque pull off the Hall of Fame Player's jersey and hand it over, unveiling No. 77 underneath. It was a fitting coda to a brilliant Black-and-Gold career, regardless of how it ended.

13

CHIEF

Of all of Johnny Bucyk's attributes, the Hall of Fame Player's backside may have been most important. Bucyk wielded his rear as a weapon, whether in using it to deliver head-over-heels hip checks or to plant himself in the slot. Regardless of its deployment, the results were unquestionable: 545 career goals as a Bruin, most of any in team history, across 21 Black-and-Gold years of play.

"John was the kind of player I didn't appreciate until I played on the same line with him," former linemate Jean Ratelle said in the book *Boston Bruins: Greatest Moments and Players*. "When I played in New York, I knew that he was good, but I didn't appreciate how much he did for the team on the ice with his knowledge and how much he did for the team off the ice."

It is not easy to determine all of Bucyk's contributions to the organization. Upon retiring in 1977–78, Bucyk never left the Bruins. Bucyk served as an analyst on WBZ Radio. He worked in the team's public relations department. He served as a goodwill ambassador, much like on-ice peer and rival Jean Beliveau did with the Canadiens. Bucyk was the team's road services coordinator, overseeing the team's travel plans and barking out departure times for the bus in the dressing room, before ceding the position after the 2014–15 season. Not many employees served one organization for 58 years like the man everybody calls Chief, all with a smile that betrayed temporary moments of portrayed gruffness.

Bucyk, an Edmonton native, played for his hometown Flyers of the Western Hockey League. The franchise was an important launchpad for future NHLers such as Glenn Hall, Bronco Horvath, and Vic Stasiuk. The latter two would reunite with Bucyk in Boston. But before that, Bucyk played for Detroit, Edmonton's varsity franchise. Bucyk showed promise with the Red Wings. During his second NHL season, Bucyk potted 10 goals in 66 games. But the left wing's skating was his biggest shortcoming, enough of a deficiency that Detroit traded him to the Bruins for Terry Sawchuk on June 10, 1957. The Wings wanted an upgrade in goal from Hall, while the Bruins had a puck-stopping asset in Sawchuk.

Bucyk accelerated his development in Boston under coach Milt Schmidt. Five days before the Bruins traded for Bucyk, they acquired Horvath from Montreal in the intraleague draft. In Boston, Bucyk and Horvath were reunited with Stasiuk, their former Edmonton teammate. Schmidt put the three forwards together on what would become the Uke Line in honor of their heritage. Bucyk and Stasiuk had roots in Ukraine. That Horvath's family was from Hungary would have to be overlooked. Together, they became the successors to the Kraut Line, the threesome their coach once centered between Woody Dumart and Bobby Bauer. Horvath

ON THIS DATE

NOVEMBER 9, 1972

Johnny Bucyk scores a goal in the Bruins' 8–3 win over Detroit, his former team. Bucyk becomes the seventh player in league history to score 1,000 career points.

controlled the puck and looked for his wingers. Stasiuk was the mucker in the danger areas. Bucyk served as the triggerman, coming off the left-side wall or parking himself in front of the net.

Bucyk scored 21 goals in his first season as a Bruin. Stasiuk also potted 21, while Horvath led the team with 30 goals. That season, Willie O'Ree made history by becoming the NHL's first black player. The Bruins lost to the Canadiens in the Stanley Cup Final. For Bucyk, it was the first of 20 straight seasons of double-digit goals. But Bucyk's consistency did not lead to results for the Bruins. The Bruins bottomed out in 1959–60, when they failed to make the playoffs for the first time since 1927. In 1960–61, Bucyk and the Bruins went 15–42–13. It was the worst record in the league, the first time the Bruins finished last since their inaugural season in 1924–25. Naturally, they failed to qualify for the postseason again.

Bucyk would not see the playoffs again until 1968, when the Canadiens swept the Bruins in four straight. But by then, Bucyk finally had the reinforcements that were missing for most of the decade. Phil Esposito, Ken Hodge, and Fred Stanfield had arrived from Chicago. Bobby Orr had submitted his rookie season. After a disappointing 18-goal season in 1966–67, Bucyk rebounded with 30 strikes and 39 assists for 69 points, then a career best. No longer could opponents train their best defensemen against Bucyk, whose former linemates had either moved on or retired. Other teams had to account for both Esposito and Bucyk, who played on separate lines. If rival coaches wanted to negate the top line of Hodge, Esposito, and Wayne Cashman, the Bruins' No. 2 line of Bucyk, Stanfield, and John McKenzie had more time and space with which to put pucks in nets.

"There's much less pressure on me this season," Bucyk told *Sports Illustrated*. "This is the first year I don't pick up a paper once a week and read that I'm about to be traded."

BEST NICKNAMES

Johnny Bucyk is of Ukrainian heritage, not North American as his nickname might hint. Bucyk earned the "Chief" tag because of the way he led the charge into the corners and used his stick like a tomahawk to pursue the puck. It was a clever nickname, back when they used to be more creative than making a play on a player's last name.

Chief had plenty of company, like Turk (Derek Sanderson), Cheesy (Gerry Cheevers), Mr. Zero (Frank Brimsek), Taz (Terry O'Reilly), Pie (John McKenzie), Nifty (Rick Middleton), Sudden Death (Mel Hill), and Grapes (Don Cherry).

In 1969–70, Bucyk finally claimed the Cup that was but a dream earlier in the 1960s. Bucyk scored 31 goals and 38 assists for 69 points, fourth most after Orr, Esposito, and McKenzie.

"Clarence Campbell made the Stanley Cup presentation and it felt great, something that can't be put into words, to receive the Cup from him," Bucyk said in *Boston Bruins: Greatest Moments and Players*. "Skating around the Boston Garden with the Stanley Cup was one of the greatest moments of my life. The fans gave us a standing ovation. A tremendous roar literally rocked the Boston Garden. My hair stood on end. It just didn't stop."

Bucyk turned in his best season in 1970–71 when he scored 51 goals, becoming only the fifth player to break the 50-goal threshold along with Esposito, Maurice Richard, Blake Geoffrion, and Bobby Hull. The Bruins fell short to the Canadiens in the playoffs. But Bucyk won his second ring in 1971–72, scoring 32 goals and 51 assists and adding 20 points in the postseason. He finished his career with 1,436 games and 1,339 points, second in both categories only to Ray Bourque. Bucyk was inducted into the Hockey Hall of Fame in 1981.

14

WILLIE O'REE
BLAZES THE WAY

The odds were against Willie O'Ree making it to the NHL, and not because he was black. It was because his right eye was just about useless.

The native of Fredericton, New Brunswick, was a promising young player. He played his junior hockey for Kitchener of the Ontario Hockey Association. There, during a game against Guelph in 1955–56, O'Ree suffered a career-threatening injury.

Teammate Kent Douglas, a strong defenseman, wound up for a slap shot from the point while O'Ree was standing in front of the net. The puck deflected off traffic and caromed into O'Ree's face. The impact broke O'Ree's nose. But that wasn't the worst damage.

"I was still conscious, but I remember I had dropped to my knees," O'Ree said in Boston Bruins: Greatest Moments and Players. "They took me to the hospital and they did surgery. I was in the hospital about four or five days, and when I opened my eyes, I could see just a light out of my good eye, and I couldn't see anything out of my right eye. And I thought I was blind."

O'Ree had lost approximately 95 percent of the sight in his right eye.

Doctors told O'Ree his hockey career was over when it was just getting started. It would have been dangerous for any player to be without the sight in one eye. It was especially so for O'Ree, a left-shot left wing. To see opponents, teammates, or puck on his right flank, O'Ree had to turn his head and body to see what was coming.

It would have been a dispiriting and premature conclusion to a career that had potential. The 5'10", 180-pound forward was not big. But he was a good skater and a smart player. He kept up with his linemates. He didn't mind battling with larger opponents. In 1955–56, O'Ree scored 30 goals and 28 assists for Kitchener. All that, however, was about to go away because of the damage Douglas' shot had done to his right eye.

It took O'Ree about eight weeks to recover. During that time, he committed himself to fulfilling his dream of playing in the NHL, regardless of his handicap. He would keep it a secret. If word got out, no team would be reckless enough to sign a player with one good eye.

Hockey, after all, was his first love. O'Ree was good enough at baseball to earn an invitation to the Milwaukee Braves' minor league camp in 1956. By then, Jackie Robinson had broken Major League Baseball's color barrier nine years earlier. The NHL, however, did not have its Robinson equivalent.

Punch Imlach didn't know about O'Ree's condition. Imlach, the future general manager of the Maple Leafs, signed O'Ree to the Quebec Aces of the Quebec Hockey League. O'Ree played well as a first-year pro, scoring 22 goals and 12 assists in 68 games despite his compromised eyesight.

During his second season with the Aces, the call he had been dreaming of finally came. During the fall of 1957, O'Ree attended training camp with the Bruins. He didn't make the team and returned to the Aces, but GM Lynn Patrick had taken notice of his speed and skill. When injuries hit the Bruins in January of 1958, Patrick needed short-term reinforcements. O'Ree would be his man. It just so happened that O'Ree was black.

On January 18, O'Ree and the Bruins visited the Montreal Forum. O'Ree had played in the signature Montreal rink before as a member of the Aces. This time, he was a third-line NHL left wing, riding alongside Larry Regan and Fleming MacKell. The Bruins beat the Canadiens 3–0. O'Ree had broken the NHL's color barrier in an understated manner, much like the way he played for the rest of his career. Robinson's entry into baseball was news around the world. O'Ree's debut did not attract the level of attention of Robinson's achievement.

"The big write-up was, BRUINS SHUT OUT HABS," O'Ree recalled to the *Boston Globe* 50 years after his groundbreaking achievement. "Nothing really mentioned about Willie O'Ree breaking the color barrier. It wasn't until I was called back that the media said, 'Oh, there's Willie O'Ree—he's the Jackie Robinson of hockey.' The name has stuck with me over the years."

O'Ree played in the back half of the home-and-home series at Boston Garden. He and the Bruins did not fare as well in his Garden debut, losing to Montreal 6–2. The Bruins returned O'Ree to Quebec after the second game. He would be back.

In 1960–61, O'Ree returned to Boston for a longer stay. The 25-year-old appeared in 43 games for the Bruins in his second go-around, scoring four goals and 10 assists. O'Ree settled into the rhythms of the city. He stayed with family in Roxbury, one of Boston's neighborhoods, and commuted to the Garden via a train line that is still running. O'Ree had good memories of living and playing in Boston. He could not say that about one of his visits to Chicago.

The Blackhawks had a forward named Eric Nesterenko. During one of Chicago's home games against the Bruins, Nesterenko, by O'Ree's recollection, approached him from the side and planted his stick in his face. O'Ree lost several teeth and his lip busted open.

"He made racial remarks at me, but it wasn't the racial remarks that set me off," O'Ree told the *Boston Globe*. "He just stood there and laughed, like, 'What's this guy gonna do? He's probably not gonna do anything.' Well, I had to make a choice right there. Either turn and skate away or fight. I hit him over the head with my stick. Cut his head open."

A brawl took place between the two clubs. After returning to the dressing room, O'Ree turned out the lights and considered leaving the league. O'Ree determined he was not going to let one player dictate his exit.

After the season, the Bruins traded O'Ree to the Canadiens. O'Ree never played a game for Montreal. The Canadiens traded O'Ree to Los Angeles of the Western Hockey League. O'Ree became a regular for the Blades, then for the San Diego Gulls, also of the WHL.

O'Ree never returned to the NHL. He didn't have to. In 45 career games, O'Ree had made a lifetime's impact on the league and the game.

15

MUSCLE AND TOUCH

am Neely played hockey on his terms. When the puck was on his stick, he steamed toward the net, shrugged off would-be defenders, and put it past the goalie. When the puck wasn't under his control, he ran over everything in a quest to hunt it down. When he didn't care for another player, he let his unfortunate opponent know with his fists. The right wing wasn't just another NHL forward. He was both violence and grace personified.

So it was not surprising to Harry Sinden that the man who almost always got his way was quite unhappy with how the sport treated him at the end.

"He had that devastating injury," Sinden said. "He was kind of mad at hockey for a few years. But his heart was always strongly there. He wanted to get back in."

On September 5, 1996, a 31-year-old Neely should have been preparing for his 14th NHL season. Instead, he put an end to his career that day because of a degenerative hip condition. He was just five strikes away from 400 career goals and one helper short of 300 assists. Given his previous rate of production, it would have taken a healthy Neely a shift or two to reach both milestones. Neely's body, however, would not allow him back on the ice.

Tears came easily to Neely's eyes as he emotionally announced his retirement:

Unfortunately, today I must face the worst-case scenario. Dr. [Bert] Zarins and the many fine medical specialists he has consulted have concluded that my right hip injury is a permanent disability which would prevent me from ever returning to professional hockey. Unlike other injuries, which I've been able to overcome to play again, there's no rehabilitation program or other surgical procedure which can help eliminate or improve my condition. I've always wanted to stay in this game as long as I could, achieving results and making positive contributions to my team. I never, ever wanted to play the game for the money or simply to go through the motions. Believe me, I loved playing in the big game. I love the competitiveness of this sport. Since the day I arrived here in Boston, I gave 100 percent to our team, my teammates, and our fans.

It was an unfortunate and unfair exit to a player who had introduced a singular style to the league. Neely defined the position of power forward: an overwhelming physical presence with fists hard enough to pound jaws, yet soft enough to pump pucks into nets.

Neely's career reached its peak in back-to-back seasons. In 1989–90, Neely scored 55 goals and 37 assists in 76 games. He could have put more goals on his resume had he not spent 117 minutes in the penalty box. In 1990–91, Neely followed it up with 51 goals and 40 assists in 69 games. His behavior was slightly better, having reduced his penalty minutes to a mere 98. In both seasons, Craig Janney served as Neely's primary disher. Janney was a skilled setup man, but it would not have taken much of a helping hand to give Neely his goals. Neely ran over everybody to track down pucks and tuck them away.

ON THIS DATE

JANUARY 3, 1996

Cam Neely and Kevin Stevens dress for the Bruins' game at Toronto's Maple Leafs Gardens. But rookie coach Steve Kasper does not give either of his forwards a single shift in a 4–4 tie. Both sit on the bench in uniform for the entire game instead of being scratched.

This was the kind of career the Bruins projected for the native of Comox, British Columbia. Their scouts loved the way he played junior hockey for the Portland Winterhawks. During his draft year, Neely scored 56 goals and 64 assists in 72 games. If the Bruins had the No. 1 pick in 1983, Sinden would not have hesitated to call Neely's name. But the Bruins had the 21st pick that year. Neely only made it to No. 9 before the Canucks, his hometown team, made him their property.

The Bruins were disappointed. But in 1986, after Neely recorded a 14–20–34 line in 73 games as a third-year pro, Vancouver made the right wing available. On June 6, 1986, the Bruins traded Barry Pederson to the Canucks for Neely and a 1987 first-round pick, which they used to draft steady defenseman Glen Wesley. It was one of the organization's biggest heists ever.

"We couldn't believe that this young junior that we coveted so much as a junior player was going to come to us through a fluke," Sinden said.

Neely's arrival in Boston coincided with the Bruins' resurgence. Neely was one of the most important players on the rosters that fell short to the powerhouse Oilers, first in 1988, then again in 1990. It was a year later, however, that one of Neely's signature moments took place.

In Game 3 of the 1991 Eastern Conference Final against Pittsburgh, Penguins defenseman Ulf Samuelsson put Neely in his crosshairs. In center ice, Samuelsson approached Neely and drove his knee into the power forward's right thigh. Then in Game 6, Neely tried to hit Samuelsson. Neely took the worst of the hit in his left knee and thigh. The collision caused the bruise in his left leg to ossify. It was the beginning of the end.

Neely played only nine games in 1991–92. The following season, he was limited to just 13 games. He wowed his teammates and opponents in 1993-94 when he powered in 50 goals in 49 games. But Neely's body could not withstand NHL pounding for much longer. Although he tried a comeback in 1998, the pain in his right hip was too much for the 33-year-old to bear.

Neely's playing career ended in disappointment. But the manner in which he changed the game in such a short window made an impression. In 2004, the Bruins retired Neely's No. 8. It was the 10th number to be retired. In 2005, he was inducted to the Hockey Hall of Fame.

Two years later, Neely returned to the Bruins as vice president. On June 16, 2010, Neely was promoted to president. Three hundred and sixty four days later, Neely lifted the Stanley Cup over his head in his hometown of Vancouver. The trophy he never touched as a player was finally his as an executive.

"Cam's career was so brilliant, and then to end so suddenly, we didn't really get to make that kind of judgment," Sinden said when asked if he considered Neely as a hockey executive upon retirement. "I'm glad it turned out that way."

16

WAR HEROES

It is possible that Bobby Bauer, the Bruins' dependable right wing, could have remained in Boston with his club instead of reporting to the Royal Canadian Air Force. According to a letter from Globe and Mail sports editor Vern DeGeer, published in the *Boston Globe* on February 21, 1942, Bauer did not have to answer his country's call because of his age. But had Bauer remained in Boston, he would have parted with linemates and longtime friends Woody Dumart and Milt Schmidt. Bauer had no intentions of doing such a thing.

"Bauer falsified his age, registering as 25 [the present draft limit], when he was actually 26," DeGeer wrote. "Bauer gave his age a twist in order to go into military service with his lifelong pals. Had he chosen—and military authorities agreed to declare him out of the draft if he produced his correct birth credentials—Bauer could have remained with the Boston Bruins. He is a recent bridegroom. But the lads had months ago agreed to enlist together. So Bauer refused to toy with the age-releasing proposal—and went along."

Bauer's actions aligned with his character. After all, Bauer was inseparable from

Dumart and Schmidt on the ice. It would be the same away from the rink.

Bauer was the oldest of the three boys from Kitchener, Ontario. As such, the right wing was the first to attract the Bruins' attention. The Maple Leafs had their eyes set on Bauer when he was playing for St. Michael's College in Toronto. Bauer also played for the St. Michael's Majors.

But Bauer and his future teammates first made their marks in their hometown. Back then, Dumart, Schmidt, and Bauer were known as the Kitchener Kids. Schmidt was a do-it-all center. Dumart was a shoot-first left wing. Bauer, while undersized at 5'6", was good at playing the puck and processing the game. They were friends first, not just on-ice teammates.

"I don't remember exactly when I first met Porky—that's what we've always called Dumart—but I must have been about 7 or 8," Schmidt told *Sports Illustrated*. "Pork was about a year and a half older than me, and big for his age, and he played defense. I didn't see so much of Bobby when I was a kid, since he lived across the river, but all of us knew each other and kept running into each other playing hockey or baseball."

In 1935, Bauer had completed his first junior season, scoring 12 goals and six assists with the Kitchener Greenshirts. On May 11, the Bruins claimed the 20-year-old Bauer from Syracuse of the International Hockey League in the interleague draft. Bauer would soon have company in Boston.

In October of 1935, Bauer attended training camp with the Bruins. The team also invited Dumart and Schmidt to camp. The previous season, Dumart scored 17 goals and 11 assists for the Greenshirts. Schmidt, as a 16-year-old, recorded 20 goals and six assists for Kitchener. Of the three, Schmidt showed the greatest promise.

ON THIS DATE

JANUARY 6, 1942

Pucks that fly into the stands usually fall in the finder's-keeper's category. But at Boston Garden, an announcement is made during the game to request fans to return any pucks that go into the crowd because of a wartime rubber shortage.

The camp was a good opportunity for the Kitchener Kids to show their stuff. On October 9, Dumart joined Bauer as a Boston employee by signing with the Bruins as a free agent. The same day, Schmidt also signed with the Bruins. None of the three made the varsity full-time in 1935-36, although Bauer and Dumart both appeared in one game. The Kitchener Kids would be best served with an apprenticeship in Providence under coach Albert "Battleship" Leduc. While coaching the Reds in 1936–37, Leduc gave the three young forwards a nickname that would stick: the Kraut Line.

"He said, 'All you fellas come from Kitchener/Waterloo,'" Schmidt recalled to the Hockey Hall of Fame. "'There's a lot of people of German descent from there. We gotta get a name for ya—the Kraut Line!' We didn't mind. It was a name that kinda stuck to us."

Before Providence, the three had not played together regularly on the same line. They would rarely be apart after leaving Providence. On March 21, 1937, Dumart, Schmidt, and Bauer skated together for the first time as Bruins. In 1937-38, all three became NHL regulars. Bauer led the Bruins with 20 goals. Schmidt and Dumart submitted identical lines of 13 goals and 14 assists each.

The Bruins finished the regular season in first place, but lost three straight games to Toronto in the playoffs.

The Kraut Line and the Bruins had better luck in 1938–39. In the playoffs, the Bruins beat the Rangers in seven games. During the series, Mel Hill earned the nickname "Sudden Death," an appropriate branding for a player who scored three overtime winners for the Bruins. In the final, the Bruins took revenge against the Maple Leafs by winning the series 4–1. The Kraut Line combined for seven goals. Frank Brimsek allowed just 18 goals in 12 games.

Two years later, the Kraut Line and Brimsek repeated their business. The Bruins dispatched the Leafs in seven games to open the playoffs. It was easy street from there. The Red Wings were no match for the mighty Bruins, who rolled to their second Cup in three seasons by sweeping them in four straight. Schmidt led the league in playoff scoring with five goals and six assists for 11 points. In Game 4, Bauer scored the Cup-clinching goal at 8:43 of the second period.

The Kraut Line was set up for more than just two Cups. All three were in the sweet spots of their careers. But they were also at the age when their services were required for something far more serious than NHL hockey. On December 9, 1941, the Bruins hosted Chicago in the first game following the declaration of war. Boston Garden was darkened during the national anthem while a spotlight was trained on the American flag. That night, the second period was delayed for approximately 45 minutes because of President Franklin Roosevelt's first wartime radio broadcast.

Two months later, the Kraut Line bid the Bruins goodbye. On February 10, 1942, they played their final game before reporting to the RCAF. The Bruins beat the Canadiens on home ice 8–1. Players from both teams lifted the three forwards onto their shoulders and carried them off the ice. Bauer recalled it as one of the most significant moments of his life.

After the war, the forwards returned to the Bruins in 1945–46. They did not stay together for long. Following a career-high 30-goal season in 1946–47, Bauer announced his retirement. He was only 32 years old. Bauer returned for one final game to honor his linemates and the Bruins. On March 18, 1952, Bauer came out of retirement on Schmidt-Dumart Appreciation Night at the Garden to play one final game. NHL president Clarence Campbell presented the Kraut Line with three gold watches. Schmidt scored his 200th career goal in the Bruins' 4–0 win over Chicago. It was the perfect way for the Kraut Line to go out.

17

AN UNLIKELY MAESTRO

There was nothing conventional about Tim Thomas. Not his career, not his goaltending style, not his personality, not his choice to celebrate a championship, not his exit from Boston.

Thomas made a living, however, of defying convention. Nobody believed the 5′11″ goalie from Flint, Michigan, would ever become a two-time Vezina Trophy winner. To most trained eyes, Thomas was an undersized and unorthodox goalie in an industry that celebrated height and proper technique.

Thomas used all those doubts as ammunition. In the end, Thomas had the last laugh.

By June of 2011, Thomas had reached the apex of his profession at 37 years of age. At Vancouver's Rogers Arena, Thomas claimed the Conn Smythe Trophy as playoff MVP, the oldest player in NHL history to win the prize. Later that month, Thomas nabbed his second Vezina Trophy as the league's best goalie.

Without Thomas, the Bruins would not have won their first Cup since 1972. He had help from fellow stars such as Zdeno Chara, Patrice Bergeron,

David Krejci, and Mark Recchi. But ultimately, the Cup was proof that an unconscious goalie can lead his team to greatness.

"He's had so many obstacles in front of him that he's overcome that it makes him a battler," said coach Claude Julien. "It makes him the perfect goaltender for our organization, because that's what we are—we're a blue-collar team that goes out, works hard, and earns every inch of the ice that you can get."

In the first round, Thomas went toe-to-toe with Montreal's Carey Price. He got the better of Price in seven games. Thomas got a breather in the second round when the Bruins swept Philadelphia.

Ray Bourque was more than happy to hand over his No. 7 to Phil Esposito so it could be retired in Esposito's honor.

Thomas had to be an ace in the Eastern Conference Final against Tampa Bay, when the up-and-coming Lightning took the Bruins to seven games. In Game 7, facing off against fellow graybeard Dwayne Roloson, Thomas was literally perfect, stopping 24 of 24 pucks in the Bruins' 1–0 win.

Thomas was airtight in Game 7. He made his best stop, however, in Game 5. In the third period, the Lightning were down 2–1. Eric Brewer wound up for a slap shot that glanced off the end boards and hopped onto the stick of Steve Downie. The Tampa forward was staring at an empty net to tie the game. But Thomas, who had been tangling with former University of Vermont classmate Martin St. Louis, dove to his right and knocked away Downie's bid with the tip of his blade.

"I have some idea about how quickly it's going to come off the boards and how much time I have to get over there," Thomas told the *Boston Globe*. "I know I don't have time to get my full body over there. The only thing I'm going to be able to make that save with is my stick."

It was Thomas at his athletic best. There have been few goalies who have been as quick and explosive or eager to use any part of his body or equipment to keep the puck out of the net.

But Thomas' stick save on Downie also represented his keen hockey sense. He was always at a disadvantage because of his height; Thomas ceded four inches, for example, to Vancouver counterpart Roberto Luongo.

Thomas compensated with his vision and brain power. He was always thinking one or two plays ahead and how he'd have to position himself for the second and third saves, not the initial stop. Thomas' style required aggressiveness to cut down angles and take away areas of the net. So when he launched out of his crease, farther than most goalies would ever dare, Thomas was scanning the rink for secondary threats and thinking about how he'd get there to shut them down.

"When I'm on top of my game, I'm reading the game very well," Thomas said. "Even when I'm not on top of my game, I'm still reading the game fairly well. A lot of that comes with experience. I think I've always had a good read for the game. But when you play as long as I have, it's one of those things that develops and makes it easier."

Thomas tried playing this way in 2009–10. It didn't work. His body wouldn't let him.

On March 4, 2010, Thomas was playing against former teammate Phil Kessel, who had moved on to Toronto. Thomas went into the splits and kicked out Kessel's breakaway bid with his right pad. Thomas made the save. But he had done some bad damage. Thomas had torn the labrum in his left hip. From then on, whenever he dropped into the butterfly, Thomas felt the injury.

Thomas lost his job to Tuukka Rask. Thomas, who had won the Vezina the previous season, didn't play at all in the playoff series against Buffalo and Philadelphia. On May 21, 2010, Thomas underwent repairs on his hip at New York's Hospital for Special Surgery. It was a significant procedure for an aging goalie.

In retrospect, it was one of the most significant procedures in the organization's history. Without it, Thomas might not have been at his peak for the 2011 Cup run.

"I'm not even thinking about last year anymore," Thomas said that summer. "It's all about coming in this year in the best physical shape absolutely possible. The easy way to put it is just playing to the best of my ability. But it's not just that. I've got something to prove. To the whole world."

The mobility and athleticism that went missing in 2010 returned postsurgery. Thomas was back employing his trademark "battlefly"

style—leaving the crease, attacking the first shot, and using his
smarts to reset for follow-up chances.

His style looked chaotic. To Thomas, it all made sense.

At Vermont, where he starred for four seasons, Thomas didn't
play with any kind of structure. All he worried about was stopping
the puck. It didn't matter how he did it, as long as he gave up fewer
goals than his opponent.

This approach—or lack of one—would not serve him well as
a pro. Quebec had picked Thomas in the ninth round of the 1994
NHL Draft. After Thomas' junior season, the franchise, which had
since relocated to Colorado, asked if he wanted to turn pro. Thomas
declined, citing his desire to earn his degree.

After graduating a year later, Thomas reported to Avalanche
training camp in Denver. He did not last long. The Avalanche had
tabbed Patrick Roy and Craig Billington as their varsity goalies.
In Hershey, their farm club at the time, they designated David
Aebischer and Randy Petruk as their AHL goalies. Thomas did
not have a place in their system. Upon his release, Thomas had a
message to then-coach Marc Crawford.

"When I left here, I told them I was going to prove them wrong,"
Thomas said during a 2008 visit to Denver. "And part of the drive
has been to do exactly that."

It was never good enough for Thomas to strive for excellence. He played with a chip on his shoulder the size of Michigan. Amid all his stops, whether in Houston, Birmingham, Hamilton, or any of the outposts he considered temporary places of employment, Thomas was determined to inform all of his ex-employers they had goofed.

By 2004–05, during one of the NHL's lockouts, Thomas was starring for Jokerit Helsinki in Finland. By the end of the season, the 30-year-old Thomas had acknowledged that his NHL opportunity would be limited to the four games he played for the Bruins in 2002–03.

Things change.

"I had actually made peace with the fact I wasn't going to get my chance," Thomas told the *Boston Globe.* "I let the dream die, so to speak. I was going to be happy playing in Finland. Then, all of a sudden, Boston stuck the carrot under my nose and I was back chasing the dream again."

In 2005–06, after signing with the Bruins, Thomas appeared in 26 AHL games for Providence. When Andrew Raycroft and Hannu Toivonen were hurt for the Bruins, the club recalled Thomas for big-league duty. Thomas had to clear waivers to land in Boston. Twenty-nine teams took a pass. Most regretted their decision.

That year, Thomas went 12–13–10 with a 2.77 goals-against average and a .917 save percentage, respectable statistics for a goalie who had never seen regular NHL play. He became a legitimate No. 1 goalie the next year, posting a 3.13 GAA and a .905 save percentage in 66 appearances.

Still, his own bosses didn't trust him. On July 1, 2007, the Bruins acquired Manny Fernandez from Minnesota for prospect Petr Kalus and a 2009 fourth-round pick. Former GM Peter Chiarelli pegged Fernandez as the starter. It didn't happen, partly because of Fernandez's wonky knee (just four appearances in 2007–08) and

Thomas' emergence. Thomas went 28-19-6 with a 2.44 GAA and a .921 save percentage, setting him up for the first of two Vezinas the following season.

While he was superhuman in 2008-09 and 2010-11, Thomas was merely very good in 2011-12, when he and the Bruins lost to the Capitals in the first round of the playoffs. By the end of the season, Thomas was spent. On June 3, 2012, Thomas declared he was done with hockey for one year. He was under contract with the Bruins for one more season. He never played for the Bruins again. He was traded to the Islanders on February 7, 2013.

"From the earliest age I can remember, I've wanted to be a hockey player," Thomas posted on his Facebook page. "I've been blessed in my life to not only be able to live that dream, but to achieve more than I ever thought possible. The singleminded focus that is necessary to accomplish a dream of this magnitude entails (by necessity) sacrifice in other areas and relationships in life. At the age of 38, I believe it is time to put my time and energies into those areas and relationships that I have neglected. That is why at this time I feel the most important thing I can do in my life is to reconnect with the three F's. Friends, Family, and Faith."

It was not the first time Thomas employed social media to deliver a surprising message. On January 23, 2012, the Bruins attended a ceremony at the White House with President Obama to celebrate their 2011 championship. Everyone was there except Thomas, who remained at the team's Washington hotel. Later that day, Thomas posted the following on Facebook:

"I believe the federal government has grown out of control, threatening the rights, liberties, and property of the people," Thomas wrote. "This is being done at the executive, legislative, and judicial level. This is in direct opposite to the Constitution and the Founding Fathers' vision for the federal government. Because I believe this, today I exercised my right as a free citizen and did not visit the White House. This was not about politics or party, as in my opinion, both parties are responsible for the situation we are in as a country. This was about a choice I had to make as an individual."

Chiarelli, who was aware of Thomas' pending decision, spoke with his goalie several times before the ceremony. The stubborn Thomas did not change his mind. It did not sit well with at least one of his fellow employees.

"[Expletive] selfish [expletive]," said a team source.

It was Thomas doing things his way. It was not out of character. He made an entire career following this approach.

18

QUICK CHANGE

Ray Bourque and the Bruins had a problem. By 1987, Bourque was eight seasons into a starry NHL career. He won the Calder Trophy as the league's best rookie in 1979–80. Bourque won the first of five Norris Trophies as the league's top all-around defenseman in 1986–87. Bourque was on a career path similar to ex-Bruin Phil Esposito, who was inducted into the Hockey Hall of Fame in 1984.

Bourque wore No. 7. It was the same number on Esposito's jersey when he was working the slot and banging in pucks. Had Bourque stayed with the digits he was originally given when he reported to his first training camp, such duplication would not have taken place.

Upon his first day of camp in 1979, No. 29 was hanging in Bourque's stall. It was the number previously worn by Bruins such as Ross Lonsberry, Doug Halward, and Joe Zanussi—players whose careers did not demand retirement of their numbers.

Bourque and No. 29 were not companions for long. By the end of camp, it was clear that the 18-year-old would be in the NHL to start the season. The Bruins determined that No. 7 would be a more fitting number for their most recent first-round pick. It was the number he wore for his NHL debut. Bourque was aware of its most famous steward.

ON THIS DATE

SEPTEMBER 17, 1985

Ray Bourque becomes co-captain with Rick Middleton. Bourque will be the NHL's longest-serving captain in NHL history until Steve Yzerman turns the trick in Detroit.

"I knew who wore that for the Bruins—a great player like Phil Esposito who won two Cups, scoring titles, and did some big things here in Boston," Bourque said. "Big personality."

At first, Bourque was apprehensive about wearing No. 7. Because of its pedigree, Bourque acknowledged the pressure it would put on his shoulders. Esposito was a legend in Boston. In hindsight, No. 7 should have been retired before Bourque even arrived, hanging next to Eddie Shore's No. 2, Lionel Hitchman's No. 3, Bobby Orr's No. 4, Dit Clapper's No. 5, John Bucyk's No. 9, and Milt Schmidt's No. 15. Esposito was front and center for the Bruins' best days, winning a pair of Cups, and scoring a league-record 76 goals in 1970–71.

If anyone did justice to a number that should have been retired, it was Bourque. There was no questioning his play or his character. But the dilemma remained.

"I never heard anything," Bourque said of controversy regarding the number. "Because things went really well for me. The fans liked how I played. Other than the press. Once in a while, they'd come up to me and ask me about the number and if I thought it should be retired. Every time I was asked, I always said, 'Yes. I think he was a great player. A legend. I didn't ask for the number.' Nothing was ever talked about with Bruins management and myself, because Harry

Sinden and Phil Esposito weren't getting along together too well. Phil was really mad at Harry for trading him to the Rangers."

By December 1987, the freeze had thawed. The Bruins targeted December 3 as the date that Esposito's number would rise to the Boston Garden rafters. Esposito, then the GM of the Rangers, would finally be acknowledged for the role he played in the Bruins' prominence.

But the issue of Bourque remained. By then, No. 7 had become just as iconic on Bourque's back as it had on Esposito's. The assumption was that Bourque would play on the Garden ice with No. 7 while Esposito's No. 7 fluttered above.

That afternoon, Bourque got a call from Terry O'Reilly. The Bruins coach was in Sinden's office. O'Reilly posed a question to Bourque.

"Mr. Sinden wants to know if you'd be willing to add a 7 to your 7 and become 77," Bourque recalled O'Reilly asking. "Then Phil Esposito can have his number retired."

Bourque said yes. Upon the defenseman's approval, the plan went into motion. Before that night's game against the Rangers, Bourque would wear No. 7 in warmups one last time. After warmups, Bourque would put on his new No. 77, then layer his old No. 7 on top.

"It was pretty wild how it happened," Bourque said. "Nobody knew except my wife, the trainers, the coaches, and Harry. That was it. No fans. No teammates. No nobody."

Before the game, Esposito walked onto the ice to start the celebration. Bourque approached Esposito. They shook hands. Bourque presented the legend his white Bruins jersey with Esposito and No. 7 on the back. Then Bourque pulled off his No. 7 one last time, twirled around, and showed Esposito his new No. 77. He gave

Esposito his old jersey as a keepsake. Nobody would wear No. 7 again.

"It's all yours," Bourque told Esposito.

Esposito was overwhelmed. As he took the microphone to address the fans, Esposito struggled to put into words how he felt about the gesture.

"What this young man did tonight is something that I'll never, ever, ever forget, no matter what happens in my life," Esposito said.

Esposito fought back tears as No. 7 was pulled up to the rafters. Bourque had done a good thing. Then again, he made a career out of such acts. On October 4, 2001, No. 77 joined No. 7 above the ice.

"I knew that was the right thing to do, because when I saw Phil Esposito's face when I did that, he was speechless for the first time ever," Bourque cracked. "Great story, lot of fun to be a part of. I think that day was real special for Phil. As it should have been."

19

TAZ

T he pursuit was modest: a Coke hand-delivered to the winner's stall. The battle, however, was intense.

It was a game of one-on-one keepaway, conducted during off days, between Terry O'Reilly and Mike Milbury. The result on the scoreboard remains unknown. But the spirit of the contest wasn't about the payoff more than the competition.

"Terry was certainly a big impression," Milbury said. "We wound up rooming together a couple years. He was first on the ice, and I was usually behind him. He was last off the ice. He was 100 percent all the time. It was hard to feel any competitive edge to your game with Terry. It was hard not to feel that way with him around."

There were other Bruins with more skill than O'Reilly. There were others who skated better. But nobody worked harder than O'Reilly. He knew no other way to play.

"If you play on a team with him," said Harry Sinden, "you better give it your all."

The number that best captured O'Reilly was 2,095—the number of penalty minutes he accumulated over 891 career games. It is the organization's high-water mark of surliness,

more than double the amount totaled by Wayne Cashman, the player O'Reilly succeeded as captain. It wasn't just that O'Reilly played angry hockey. He was so competitive that his in-your-face attitude regularly manifested in his gloves dropping to the ice.

"If he had one flaw," wrote Don Cherry in *Straight Up and Personal: The World According to Grapes*, "it was a vicious temper."

The Bruins thought well enough of O'Reilly's play as an amateur that they drafted him 14th overall in 1971. The Bruins were so loaded that they didn't initially think they needed the forward's services for some time. In 1971–72, while the Bruins were roaring toward their second Stanley Cup in three seasons, O'Reilly served his apprenticeship with the Braves, recording nine goals, eight assists, and 134 penalty minutes in 60 games. He was called up for one game with the big club. The effect of skating alongside legends helped O'Reilly understand the gravity of being a Bruin.

The Bruins would require O'Reilly's pit-bull presence sooner rather than later. Derek Sanderson and John McKenzie were among the NHL stars that bolted for the World Hockey Association in 1972. Their departures gave O'Reilly his break. He did not intend to waste it.

In 1972–73, his first full NHL season, O'Reilly scored five goals and 22 assists and recorded 109 penalty minutes in 72 games. The 21-year-old believed he had joined a team that would continue its chase of multiple Cups. Instead, O'Reilly's time in the league was beginning just as the Bruins' championship window was closing. Bobby Orr's health was at risk with every game he played. Phil Esposito would be traded in 1975. Gerry Cheevers went to the WHA.

It was up to O'Reilly, now better known as Taz, to bridge the eras from Big Bad Bruins to Lunchpail AC. He did so with a flourish. In 1977–78, with Don Cherry as his coach, O'Reilly led the Bruins in scoring with 90 points (29 goals and 61 assists). He also blazed the trail with a team-high 211 penalty minutes. He was only the second player in NHL history to lead his team in points and penalty minutes in the same season. By then, O'Reilly had turned his skating, perhaps his biggest liability early in his career, into one of his assets. Because of his frenzied approach, not many opponents wanted to get in O'Reilly's way when he revved up his wheels to highway speed.

At no time was O'Reilly more dangerous that season than in the second round of the playoffs against Philadelphia. The Flyers were in the midst of being the Broad Street Bullies, the meanest and surliest bunch of players in the league. O'Reilly, however, did not back down from the Flyers' intimidation. The Bruins booted the musclebound Flyers from the playoffs 4–1, despite the best attempts by hard men such as Mel Bridgman or Rick Lapointe to do damage to O'Reilly's face.

"I wonder if even the Bruins realize how good O'Reilly really is," Flyers coach Fred Shero told *Sports Illustrated*. "I know that the rest of the world doesn't understand that O'Reilly is one of the best players in the world. He's much like Bobby Clarke in that he never stops giving second effort. Sometime soon—like right now—I've got to come up with a line that can handle O'Reilly. A line, I said, not just one player."

O'Reilly's ferocity brought the Bruins close to the Cup. But his teams were never stocked with enough talent to win it all. After taking down the Flyers in 1978, the Bruins lost to the Canadiens in the final 4–2. The following year, O'Reilly submitted another solid season: 26–51–77 and 205 penalty minutes in 80 games. The Bruins took care of Pittsburgh in four straight games in the first round of the playoffs. They were less than a period away from finally slaying the Montreal ghosts in the second round. But the Bruins were caught with too many men on the ice, which led to Guy Lafleur and overtime and Yvon Lambert and all the heartache involved in one of the franchise's most heartbreaking moments.

"They made the call and the rest is history," Milbury said. "There were a lot of tears shed that night. They were the more talented group, but we were the better team for that series. We [expletive] up. We have to live with that."

Perhaps fittingly, O'Reilly's final two seasons ended with first-round exits against Montreal. Upon O'Reilly's retirement, Sinden put it best when thinking about a lineup without No. 24.

"I've dreaded this day coming," Sinden told the *Boston Globe* during O'Reilly's retirement press conference. "I've lived in fear of what it would be like to face an NHL season without Terry O'Reilly."

O'Reilly would have the last laugh on his archrival in 1988, when he was in his second season as Bruins coach. That year, O'Reilly's team finally ended its 45-year streak of shame by beating the Canadiens in the playoffs. He was the right coach to pull off the trick.

20

THE PERPETUAL STUDENT

Things changed in a big way for Patrice Bergeron in 2007. By then, the former second-round draft pick had played in the NHL for three seasons and been an AHLer during the 2004–05 lockout. In 229 big-league games, Bergeron had scored 69 goals and 113 assists for 182 points, a very good start for the then-22-year-old center. Some fellow draftees from the class of 2003 had yet to play in the NHL.

But Bergeron was still not sure of who he was or the type of NHLer he wanted to become. As a fifth-year pro, two things helped Bergeron figure out his destiny. One of them nearly ended his career.

On October 27, 2007, in his 10th game for first-year coach Claude Julien, Bergeron chased after a puck in the offensive zone. As Bergeron approached the puck, Philadelphia defenseman Randy Jones belted the center from behind and drove him face-first into the end boards. The impact of the collision knocked Bergeron out. He lay motionless on the ice. Bergeron had suffered a major concussion. Medical personnel took him off the ice on a stretcher and drove him to nearby Massachusetts General Hospital.

At the time of his accident, Bergeron was in his first month of playing for his third NHL coach. He broke into the league under Mike Sullivan. In 2006–07, Dave Lewis took over the bench. That year, Bergeron averaged 0.91 points per game, which remains the highest offensive output of his career. But he was also on the ice for far too many opposing goals, a point of embarrassment for a player who had always been mindful of defensive stoutness.

In 2007, Julien replaced Lewis. Bergeron had played for Julien in the 2006 World Championship. Bergeron enjoyed the structure with which Julien coached. He had an even better view of Julien's style upon his arrival in Boston. One of Julien's first tasks was to illuminate the 200-foot game for Bergeron and how commitment to three-zone play could turn him into a more polished player.

"The way that he was explaining it and preaching about the game, I realized I needed to get even better in that aspect," Bergeron said. "I wanted to be a guy he could rely on in all situations."

Playing center in Julien's system would require a lot of heavy lifting. In the defensive zone, the center has to support his defensemen down low. He has to be in position to cut off passes from down low to the point. He has to be available as the primary outlet option when defensemen gain control of the puck. There is a lot of skating, checking, and thinking. These elements had always been in Bergeron's sweet spot.

"Even growing up, I wasn't happy when I was getting scored on or missing an assignment defensively," Bergeron said. "For me, it was always hockey. Hockey was always defense and offense. It wasn't just scoring goals. So it wasn't that hard for me to go that way—go in the direction of being a real two-way player."

Processing the game came naturally for Bergeron. As a 5-year-old in Quebec City, Bergeron's introduction to hockey involved sitting in the net while his teammates skated around the ice. He liked watching and learning. After two months of sitting and watching, Bergeron emerged from the net, joined the play, and became the best player on the ice.

"He was learning," Gerard Cleary, Bergeron's father, told the *Boston Globe*. "Patrice has always been learning by looking. So, I am sure he was sitting there and learning how to skate. In his mind, [when] he knows how to do it, he [does] it. Yes, unbelievable, but it's Patrice. He is always the guy that wants to learn, who wants to be the best. And I think he is doing well."

While it wasn't an early-career reboot, learning under Julien was a pivot point for Bergeron. Had the Bruins not changed coaches when they did, who knows whether Bergeron would have developed into a dominant two-way center. And who knows, had the outcome of his collision been any worse, whether his career would have continued at all.

Bergeron's life turned upside down. He had headaches. He was tired. He was sensitive to light. He couldn't focus. Dizziness, nausea, and lightheadedness were regular intrusions. Despite resuming on-ice workouts by the end of the season and during the first round of the playoffs, Bergeron didn't play again in 2007–08. In 2008–09, Bergeron scored eight goals and 31 assists in 64 games, missing 15 games because of a second concussion, this time when he collided with future teammate Dennis Seidenberg, then playing for Carolina.

The injuries changed the way Bergeron played. In battle situations, especially along the boards, Bergeron was more mindful of his surroundings. He was also more grateful of two things: good health and employment in a game he had always enjoyed.

"It made me appreciate it even more," Bergeron said. "When you're away from it for so long, you kind of realize that you miss it a lot. It's what you want to do."

By 2009–10, Bergeron started to reconnect the pieces he had started to assemble upon Julien's arrival and that Jones had scattered. Bergeron led the team in scoring with 19 goals and

<u>ON THIS DATE</u>

APRIL 13, 2006

Patrice Bergeron scores two goals against Montreal. He becomes the youngest player in Bruins history (20 years, 262 days) to score 30 goals.

33 assists for 52 points. He drew most of the hardest defensive assignments. He won 58 percent of his faceoffs.

Bergeron continued to elevate his performance in 2010–11. Julien regularly deployed Bergeron between Brad Marchand and Mark Recchi as a two-way threesome that could score and hold the line against top competition. In the regular season, Bergeron scored 22 goals and 35 assists. He had a scare in the playoffs when a Claude Giroux thump in the second round left him with a concussion. But Bergeron shook off the injury and scored the winning goal in Game 7 of the Stanley Cup Final against Vancouver.

The following year, voters finally recognized Bergeron for his play away from the puck when they awarded him the first of three Selke Trophies as the league's best defensive forward. By 2015–16, Bergeron was at the peak of his game. The 30-year-old, with Marchand being a fixture on his left flank, was the team's most important player. As usual, he played against every top line. He took every important faceoff. He killed penalties. He helped lift the power play into one of the most powerful attacks in the league as the bumper, the man in the middle of the formation tasked to do everything—shoot, distribute the puck, and relieve pressure from his teammates.

On January 19, 2016, Bergeron scored a goal in the Bruins' 4–1 win over Montreal. With the goal, his 591st point, Bergeron passed Cam Neely for ninth place on the team's all-time scoring list.

"You never stop being appreciative of him," Julien said. "You get the same thing out of him every night and more. He's not only the best two-way player in the league. He's also our leading scorer. He's taken all the biggest draws there are in a game for us. We can go on and on and on. That's just one of those guys who's going to be recognized for a long time after he's done playing as well. He's building himself into one of those players that people will remember for a long time."

The day after every game, Bergeron will watch every shift he's taken. He'll review the plays that worked and others where things were off—positioning, stick placement, a wrong read. He'll watch opposing centers to study faceoff tendencies. There is always work to be done.

21

DYNAMITE
DIT

here was no doubting Guy Lapointe's credentials. The hard-hitting, do-it-all defenseman won the Stanley Cup six times as a member of Montreal's juggernaut in the 1970s. He would be named to the Hockey Hall of Fame in 1993. His record of 28 goals in 1974–75 is still the high-water mark for Montreal defensemen in one season.

But when Lapointe signed with the Bruins in 1983, he had to trade in his usual No. 5 after several games. The Bruins acknowledged that while Lapointe had made his mark on the league while wearing No. 5 in Montreal, the number did not belong on anyone else's Black-and-Gold jersey aside from Dit Clapper.

After all, Clapper had done a lot of things for the Bruins. In 1927–28, his first season in Boston, the 20-year-old Clapper made his NHL debut as a right wing. Coach Art Ross shortly considered Clapper on defense. But Clapper returned to right wing and found a home as a linemate to Cooney Weiland and Dutch Gainor. The threesome became so good that teammates, rivals, and fans dubbed them the "Dynamite Line," one of the first groups in league history to merit a designation.

Then for the second half of his career, Clapper moved back to defense. Clapper and Eddie Shore gave the Bruins a feared 1–2 punch on the back end. Shore was the surly, brutish, take-no-prisoners bull on skates. Clapper, in contrast, applied his strength

ON THIS DATE
NOVEMBER 27, 1946

Dit Clapper plays in his first game of the season in a 5–2 win over the Rangers. By doing so, Clapper becomes the first player in league history to play in 20 seasons.

and skill in less violent ways. Shore was the gregarious and controversial version of Babe Ruth. Clapper played the part of Lou Gehrig—understated, dependable, and industrious. In 1945, Clapper became a player-coach, the first and last in team history.

"Dit was the type of player who would skate over and introduce himself cordially to a new referee or opponent, and who had built a reputation around the league as a tough-but-clean competitor," wrote Stewart Richardson and Richard LeBlanc in *Dit: Dit Clapper and the Rise of the Boston Bruins.*

But the quality that set Clapper apart from his peers was his longevity. For 20 years, Clapper went about his business for the Bruins, both at right wing and defense. In 1929, Clapper won his first Stanley Cup. Twelve years later, he won his third. Clapper is the only Bruin to win three championships (1929, 1939, 1941). He was the NHL's first player to play 20 seasons, 14 of which he served as team captain. The latter was a team record that was only broken by Ray Bourque. Only eight other players in league history have played 20 or more seasons with the same team. The 6'2", 200-pound Clapper was one of his era's thoroughbreds—tall, thick, and resilient.

"Wonder what the longest span of playing years is in the NHL? Dit must be giving it quite a tussle by now," the *Boston Globe*'s Jerry Nason wrote on December 22, 1943. "Hockey's a fast game, tough on the legs. A fellow has to be really a superman to travel 17 years as both a forward and a defenseman in pro hockey. All told, Dit has played more than two decades, and you can't do that and spend your time horsing around nights."

Clapper started his professional career with the Boston Tigers of the Canadian-American Hockey League. Clapper would not last long with the Tigers. The Bruins took note of Clapper and signed him in 1927. Clapper did not need much time to adapt to the NHL.

Clapper's best season was in 1929–30. Before the season, the league approved the use of the forward pass in all three zones. The Bruins, more than any other team, were best equipped to take advantage of the rule change because of their talented top line. That year, Clapper scored 41 goals and 20 assists as the team's No. 1 right wing.

Given the rate of his offensive production, Clapper should have played his entire career up front. But later in his career, the Bruins decided his talents were better served on defense. Clapper didn't disappoint. For three straight seasons from 1939 to 1941, Clapper was named a First Team All-Star because of how stoutly he defended.

In 1941, with Weiland, his former center, behind the bench, Clapper helped the powerhouse Bruins to their third Cup. By then, Shore, Tiny Thompson, and Gainor were gone. The new generation of Bruins, with Frank Brimsek in goal and the Kraut Line of Woody Dumart, Milt Schmidt, and Bobby Bauer leading the attack, was taking over. Clapper served as the bridge between the eras. It was no surprise that upon his retirement, the Bruins considered Clapper a no-brainer to elevate from player-coach to full-time bench boss.

Clapper was originally expected to retire after 1945–46, his 19th NHL season. Even the sturdy Clapper had become slowed by injuries. But Clapper returned for his 20th because of an injury to Jack Crawford. Clapper played in only six games in his final season, but the Bruins made it a memorable one. He played his final game on February 12, 1947, and beat the Rangers at Boston Garden 10–1. Not only did the Bruins retire his number that night, but the Hockey Hall of Fame declared Clapper to be its latest entrant. Clapper was named to the Hall of Fame before even Shore, who was considered to be the driver of the Bruins' success. He was one of only seven players who did not have to wait the mandatory three post-retirement years to be considered for entry. Clapper was that good.

"He learned a lot watching and practicing," Ross told the *Boston Globe*. "That always has been one of Dit's biggest assets, his ability to absorb lessons from others."

22

CHEESY

In the summer of 1965, the Bruins were searching for a goalie. They considered the NHL's intraleague draft that year as the opportunity to find some help between the pipes. The Bruins looked at Toronto as the best target to raid.

The Maple Leafs had talent in goal. In 1964–65, Johnny Bower and Terry Sawchuk stabilized the position. The Leafs had a third young goalie in their system: 24-year-old Gerry Cheevers. Because of the occupied net in Toronto, Cheevers had trouble cracking the Leafs' roster. He had appeared in just two career NHL games before that season.

Toronto did not want to part with the young goalie. He had played some games at forward. The Leafs tried to classify Cheevers as such before the draft. Neither the Bruins nor the league bought it. Toronto had to expose Cheevers as a goalie in the draft. The Bruins were happy to make the claim.

It did not take long for the Bruins to learn that Cheevers applied some of the thinking and athleticism he learned as a skater into his craft in the net. Where most goalies of his time stayed close to home, Cheevers liked to wander. He was good at it.

After the 2004–05 lockout, the NHL introduced the trapezoid behind each net. Because goalies had become so good at playing the puck, they were forbidden from touching it outside the trapezoid. In retrospect, Cheevers was one of the first goalies to begin the process of improving how puck stoppers handled the puck.

"He came in, and to me, he transformed the way you played goal," said Harry Sinden. "He handled the puck as well as most defensemen. He challenged every shooter. He body-checked people. He was unbelievable. After a few years with him, I thought, *Maybe he is a forward*. There were a number of goaltenders that came into the league in the years following Gerry and along with him who had the same style."

Cheever's swashbuckling style was a perfect fit in Boston. He quickly made his bosses understand they made the right call in acquiring him from Toronto. In 1967, the goalie once made expendable by Bower and Sawchuk with the Maple Leafs found himself on the other side. Cheevers, Ed Johnston, and Bernie Parent were the three Boston goalies in 1966–67. Following that season, the Bruins kept Cheevers and Johnston in the expansion draft and let Parent go to Philadelphia.

Cheevers and Johnston helped spark the Bruins' revival. Cheevers backstopped the Bruins to Stanley Cups in 1970 and 1972. In 1970, Cheevers was in net for Bobby Orr's Cup–winning goal against St. Louis. Two years later, Cheevers blanked the Rangers to help his team clinch its second Cup in three seasons.

"Never have I seen the puck go by me so many times without going in. That's what I remember about that game," Cheevers said. "They had a two-man advantage for two minutes in the second period. The puck must have gone by me 20 times and never went in. I had a lot of good luck that day."

The Bruins didn't ask Cheevers to steal games. He didn't need to. The loaded Bruins usually controlled both the puck and the pace of play. Cheevers, always a master of self-deprecation, knew how talented his teammates were.

"I was not scared in that situation, because [the puck] never hit me," Cheevers cracked about facing his star-studded team in practice. "They scored all the time."

Cheevers became better known in Boston and around the league not because of his puck-stopping prowess but because of his protection. Cheevers was the mischievous type. He didn't enjoy practice. So one day, when practice wasn't going so well, Cheevers took a puck to the face. His mask kept the puck from doing any damage. But Cheevers bailed on the session and retired to the dressing room.

"I went into the dressing room and was having some refreshments. I'm not talking out of school, so you know what I'm talking about," Cheevers said.

Sinden didn't care for Cheevers' exit. The fiery coach demanded Cheevers return to the ice. Trainer John "Frosty" Forristall came up with an idea. Forristall drew a stitch-like slash on Cheevers' previously snow-white mask to signify where the puck might have dug into his flesh. With that first stroke of artwork, Cheevers and Forristall had created one of the signature pieces of equipment in NHL history. The mask became its own character as Cheevers updated it with stitch after stitch until it became a jagged collection of would-be wounds. Jacques Plante, the first goalie to wear facial protection, may be Cheevers' only rival in terms of iconic masks.

"I can't let you go out like that," Cheevers, during a 2015 ceremony at Boston's Sports Museum, recalled Forristall telling him. "So he took a magic marker and painted the stitches on the mask. That's how it all started. I don't think I'd be here if it wasn't for the mask."

BRUINS AND THEIR MASKS

After 2009–10, Tim Thomas ditched his previous Black-and-Gold mask. He went with a white-and-gray piece for the following season. Thomas led the charge, winning the Vezina and Conn Smythe en route to backstopping the Bruins to the Cup. On the chin, Thomas went with his TT trademark logo. The crown of the mask matched the design of a pendant Thomas wore around his neck. On the back, Thomas chose the phrase, "Don't Tread On Me." Unlike his peers, who opted for the cat's-eye design, Thomas preferred vertical bars on his cage.

Other sharp designs: Andy Moog and the gold growling bear; Hannu Toivonen's mask honoring Ray Bourque, Larry Bird, David Ortiz, and Tedy Bruschi; and Steve Shields' modern tribute to Cheevers' stitches.

Cheevers left the Bruins after the second Cup when he signed with Cleveland of the World Hockey Association, the league that tripled his salary. Cheevers returned to Boston in 1976, splitting time with Gilles Gilbert. Upon retirement, Cheevers became coach on July 7, 1980. Cheevers coached in 376 games, fifth most in team history, before Sinden fired him on February 13, 1985. The loss of Cheevers' job came with a significant consolation. Later that year, Cheevers was inducted into the Hockey Hall of Fame.

Sinden later credited the innovative Cheevers as being one of the first coaches to deploy a version of the neutral-zone trap, which he devised to kill penalties.

"Nothing is better than playing," Cheevers told the *Boston Globe*. "That's not 99 percent true—it's 100 percent true. But, if you can't play and you want to stay in the game, there are other avenues. I don't think coaching is the most desirable one, but...I had a good record, and I am proud of that."

23

THE
GIANT

There is a reason Zdeno Chara, at 6'9", is the tallest player ever to make it to the NHL. The league is not welcoming to players of Chara's height.

The game is always becoming faster. General managers are not as discriminating against small, quick, and agile players as they once were. Behemoths of Chara's size have a lot of working parts that have to flow in sync together.

But Chara has always made it a point to stay ahead of the curve, regardless of the limitations his body has placed on his skill set.

"There is only so much you can do as a 6'9" guy on the ice with being agile, the quickness, the agility to make these plays," Chara said. "Naturally, you are not going to be as flashy or as sexy on the ice as players like Erik Karlsson or Duncan Keith."

Chara's size has always been his greatest asset. Opponents look at his frame, reach, and 65-inch-long stick, then shudder at the thought of approaching the Bruins captain. All those elements combine to make the left side of the defensive zone a pit of offensive quicksand. Chara can swat the puck off a forward's blade with a quick flick of his

stick. If an attacker breaches the perimeter of his stick, Chara uses his positioning to steer him away from the dangerous areas of the ice. If an opponent advances past those safeguards, the biggest and strongest player in the league flexes his muscles and bullies him out of the way. Chara's patch of ice has always been where offense goes to die.

It wasn't easy for him to earn that piece of real estate.

Because of his size, Chara was always the circus sideshow. Even in his hometown of Trencin, Slovakia, Chara never advanced to the varsity roster of Dukla, the local powerhouse. The teenage Chara moved to Czech Republic to play for Sparta Praha in Prague. There, an 18-year-old Chara had to grow up fast—live on his own, cook for himself, clean his clothes, and try to draw eyeballs halfway across the world.

The Islanders were one of the teams that saw Chara's potential. In 1996, they drafted him in the third round, purely as a long-term project. It would take time and practice not just for Chara to grow into his body, but to learn the North American game. After being drafted, Chara's first port of call was in Prince George, an outpost in British Columbia. As the foreigner with the funny name and freakish body, Chara soon became the target of musclebound opponents in the rough-and-tumble Western Hockey League. Chara did not back down.

Chara made his NHL debut on November 19, 1997. One of his teammates was Doug Houda, who was in charge of his shifts for 10 seasons as the Bruins assistant coach responsible for running the defense. His opponents included a current team president (Brendan Shanahan, Toronto) and general manager (Steve Yzerman, Tampa Bay). It was the first of four seasons on Long Island for Chara until June 23, 2001. That day, the Islanders traded Chara with Bill Muckalt

SMOKING SHOT

In January of 2012, Zdeno Chara returned to Ottawa, where he made his home from 2001 to 2006, to participate in the All-Star Game. It was a pleasant homecoming. During the skills competition, Chara hammered a shot that peaked at 108 mph. It remains the fastest shot ever recorded during the semi-regular skills contest.

That Chara set the standard is no surprise. He has perpetually been among the league's strongest players. As such, Chara wields a 65-inch-long stick—he's used the Warrior and Easton brands—that is as rigid as a telephone pole.

Only the net was the victim that night. But plenty of opponents have felt the pain of Chara's ripper. On April 4, 2011, Chara broke then–Rangers captain Ryan Callahan's leg with a slap shot.

and a first-round pick (it would become ace pivot Jason Spezza) to Ottawa for Alexei Yashin.

The trade turned into one of the best deals Ottawa ever made. The Senators saw more in Chara than a one-dimensional defenseman. Chara still did the defensive heavy lifting for his new team. Wade Redden was the primary offensive catalyst from the blue line. But the Senators allowed Chara to join the attack, pinch down the walls, and see time on the power play, where he could take advantage of his lethal slap shot.

"That's when everything changed," Chara said. "I was able to jump up in the plays. I started to play on the power play, using my shot more and more. Ottawa was where the offensive part of my game came in and I started I to be known more as a two-way defenseman instead of just a stay-at-home defenseman."

By 2005–06, Chara was playing some of his best hockey. He scored 16 goals and 27 assists for a career-high 43 points. That season, the game shifted in a direction that was not conducive to Chara's game.

Following the 2004–05 lockout, which Chara spent in Sweden, the NHL eliminated the red line. The league cracked down on obstruction penalties. It opened a figurative window on the game to let in some fresh air and enliven offense. This could have been the first step toward making defensemen like Chara obsolete. The rule changes claimed some players. Chara adapted his game. He made sure to stay atop his skating and not depend so much on his physicality. Chara became better at a pivot point where he could have gotten worse.

"That pretty much sorted out who was able to stay in the league and who was forced to leave, based on the ability to skate, make plays, and making these adjustments," Chara said. "The whole purpose of increasing scoring and the speed of the game—that was a major, major change. Of my 20 years, that was the major one."

He was also on the last year of his contract. When Peter Chiarelli, Ottawa's assistant GM, landed the top job in Boston, signing Chara was atop his priority list. On July 1, 2006, the Bruins signed Chara to a five-year, $37.5 million blockbuster. Chara would become the foundation of the Bruins' rebuild.

Things didn't start out smoothly for Chara in Boston. The Bruins finished in 13th place during his first Black-and-Gold season. In retrospect, amid a diminished roster, Chara tried to do too much. He had always been a better player when he focused on his assets.

When Claude Julien replaced Dave Lewis in 2007–08, Chara's game became more robust. Julien's marching orders to Chara emphasized the shutdown component of occupying his area, wielding his stick, and making simple plays to shuttle the puck up the ice. During Julien's first season, Chara scored a career-high 51 points. Julien also gave Chara the green light to fight, which he was forbidden to do under Lewis. Chara picked his spots, given that he was important chewing up time on the ice instead of icing his knuckles in the penalty box for five minutes. But when he dropped his gloves, he made the scraps count. On October 25, 2007, Chara made a mess of Chicago heavyweight David Koci's face in a one-sided beatdown.

Chara's strength had always made him one of the most feared players in the league. On March 8, 2011, it ended an opponent's season. Chara and Montreal left wing Max Pacioretty engaged in a second-period race for the puck. Chara checked Pacioretty into the edge of the glass between the Bell Centre benches. Pacioretty suffered a concussion and a broken vertebra. Montreal fans called 911. Chara became the subject of a criminal investigation, which was later dismissed. The NHL responded by curving the straight edge of the glass to reduce impact of subsequent collisions. Unwittingly, Chara had changed the game.

Pacioretty was unavailable to play against the Bruins later that season in the opening round of the playoffs. Chara missed one game himself because of an illness. But Chara and his teammates rallied from an 0–2 deficit to beat the Canadiens in the opening round. Chara and Dennis Seidenberg, united as a shutdown pair, helped sweep the Flyers in the second round.

Fourteen games later, Chara was lifting the Stanley Cup over his head in Vancouver. The grind of the run had taken so much out of Chara that he nearly fell over because of the trophy's weight. Fatigue, however, was not going to diminish the happiness of achieving a lifelong goal.

The Cup, after all, has been the focus of a man whose interests could have pulled him elsewhere. While he was a Senator, he studied financial planning at Ottawa's Algonquin College. In 2015, Chara earned his real estate license. He speaks Slovak, English, Czech,

German, Italian, Polish, Russian, and Swedish. But Chara has applied his energy into making himself the best shutdown defenseman in Bruins history.

"I'm planning to continue to play, play at a high level, and do whatever it takes," said Chara, who is under contract through 2018, when he will be 41. "If you really look back over the course of the years, seasons, and games, not many guys were able to make the changes and adjustments on a number of occasions throughout 20 years. It takes a lot of work, a lot of willingness to make those changes and adjustments. I'll always look at it as I always want to get better. I always want to improve. No matter what type of game or style or system I'll be in, I'll do whatever it takes."

24

BRUINS TRADE THE FRANCHISE

On Nov. 30, 2005, Joe Thornton was out to dinner in Boston with his parents, who were visiting from London, Ontario. By the meal's conclusion, Thornton, the Bruins' No. 1 pick in 1997, was a San Jose Shark. Two nights later, Thornton was doing his usual dishing thing, recording two assists against Buffalo in his San Jose debut.

Thornton's life changed. So did that of the Bruins.

"It was very difficult," then-GM Mike O'Connell told the *Boston Globe*. "Like a trade of any kind like this, it's tough. He's been with us, we drafted him, he's a good kid. But when your team isn't going in the right direction, you've got to try to get it going the right way. This deal, we feel, is going to get us going in the right direction."

O'Connell and his colleagues were wrong. Brad Stuart, Marco Sturm, and Wayne Primeau, the collective return for Thornton, did not help the Bruins make the playoffs. They finished in 13th place. On March 25, 2006, before their non-postseason fate was sealed, O'Connell was fired and replaced by interim GM Jeff Gorton. O'Connell's ouster marked a significant segment on the organizational rebuild. The souring of the Thornton trade played a big part in O'Connell's firing.

That's because Thornton shrugged off the trade, became San Jose's top center, and won the Hart Trophy. Between the two clubs, Thornton scored 29 goals and 96 assists for 125 points, good enough

ON THIS DATE
JANUARY 11, 2006

Joe Thornton plays in his first game in Boston following the trade to San Jose. He doesn't make it a period, as he is tossed at 5:13 of the first for checking good friend Hal Gill from behind.

to pace the league in scoring. Thornton turned into the player the Bruins determined he would not become.

At first, the Bruins had high hopes for the talented pivot. Ironically, in 1996–97, the Bruins and Sharks clashed in a fight to finish as the league's worst team. The Bruins were better than the Sharks at losing. The Bruins ended the year with 61 points, one fewer than the Sharks. It gave the Bruins the privilege to draft Thornton first overall. There wasn't much debate that Thornton would go first overall.

During his draft year, Thornton showed he was capable of being a franchise player. In 59 games for the OHL's Sault Ste. Marie Greyhounds, Thornton piled up 122 points. He could shoot and score. He could protect the puck from a rhinoceros. He could blend a big man's power game with the skill and finesse of a smaller and slicker player.

"He's been a great player for two years for us," Greyhounds coach Joe Paterson told the *Boston Globe*. "It's not too often that a player who is 6'4" and 200 pounds and is only 17 years of age has as much coordination and as much hockey sense as he has. He's a tremendous athlete and he's going to have a great future in the National Hockey League. He's an apple-pie type of kid. He's going to be a great person for a team to market him and use as an ambassador for their team at the next level. Right now, the NHL has to be excited as a whole. It has a great athlete like Mario Lemieux probably going to retire and maybe Thornton can be one of the two or three who comes in with so much upside as a player. I'm not saying he's going to be a Lemieux, but whoever drafts him is going to be a very fortunate franchise."

Never had the Bruins been so happy to be so lousy. They jumped at the chance to pick the curly-haired kid first overall. Seven picks later, the Bruins drafted Sergei Samsonov. The two teenagers, who made the varsity roster that fall, were supposed to be the team's foundational pieces for the rest of their careers.

The Bruins had an idea, however, that Thornton's entry to the NHL would take time. While Samsonov ripped up the league for 22 goals and 25 assists in his rookie season, winning the Calder Trophy, Thornton was nowhere near as ripe. Then-coach Pat Burns took a firm approach with his prodigy. Burns regularly played the future No. 1 center on his fourth line. Thornton averaged only 8:05 of ice time per game, scoring three goals and four assists in 55 appearances.

Thornton's development proceeded accordingly. In his second season, Thornton scored 16 goals and 25 assists while missing just one game. In 1999–2000, Thornton led the Bruins in scoring with 23 goals and 37 assists for 60 points. Thornton had his best season in 2002–03. By then, wearing No. 19 instead of the No. 6 given to him as a rookie, Thornton put up a 36–65–101 line while centering fellow widebodies Mike Knuble and Glen Murray. Opposing teams could not do much against the threesome once they controlled the puck except get out of their way.

Despite his growth, the Bruins were not satisfied with their captain. In 2003–04, the Bruins should have rolled over the Canadiens in the first round of the playoffs, especially after grabbing a 3–1 series lead. Instead, Montreal roared back and ended the Bruins' season. Thornton, playing with torn rib cartilage, didn't score a point. There was something eluding Thornton, be it fire or grit or an unidentifiable quality that kept him from becoming one of the league's dominant players.

Despite their reservations, the Bruins signed Thornton to a three-year, $20 million extension following the 2004–05 lockout. At 26 years old, Thornton was still in the sweet spot of his career. Upon the lockout's conclusion, the league cracked down on holding, interference, and hooking—the ways, in other words, that opponents often tried to diminish Thornton's puck-protection game. With the game opening up postlockout, Thornton should have been in a position to thrive.

But the Bruins sputtered at the start of 2005–06. Andrew Raycroft struggled in goal. Brian Leetch's best days were behind him. First-year Bruins such as Alexei Zhamnov, Brad Isbister, Dave Scatchard, and Tom Fitzgerald did not do enough to help their new club.

On November 29, 2005, the Bruins lost to the Devils 3–2. They lost in a bad way. With just 32 seconds left in regulation, Thornton lost a defensive-zone faceoff cleanly to John Madden. One second later, Alex Mogilny slipped the game-winning goal past Raycroft, even before Thornton had time to recover from the lost draw. As the Devils celebrated, Thornton stared at the Continental Airlines Arena ceiling in disbelief. One night later, he was an ex-Bruin.

Thornton thrived in San Jose. As teammates with Patrick Marleau, the player who went right behind him in the 1997 draft, Thornton became one of the best centers of his generation. Thornton and the Sharks made nine straight playoff appearances before failing to make the postseason in 2014–15. He won Olympic gold with Team Canada in 2010. He became the 33rd player in NHL history to record 1,300 points. He's done it all with his trademark smile on his face.

25

CASH MONEY

B y 1980, the Islanders were ready for liftoff. That spring, they would hoist the first of four straight Stanley Cups, identifying themselves as one of the NHL's premier dynasties of all time. The Bruins had the misfortune of running into the juggernauts in the second round of the playoffs. They did not intend to bow out without a fight—literally.

At the time, Wayne Cashman was 34 years old. Cashman, an up-and-comer during the glory years of 1970 and 1972, had some salt in his beard by then. But when Garry Howatt engaged Cashman in a fight-filled Game 2, the aging Bruin did not back down. Cashman and Howatt tangled twice in a first period where the Bruins and Islanders combined for 248 penalty minutes, a league record.

"He suckered him," Mike Milbury recalled. "Cash came back to school on him. It was a vicious series. We gave them everything they could handle. The point was Cashman was a warrior. We knew it. He didn't gloat about it. He didn't brag about it. He thought he'd do it when he had to do it."

Milbury knew firsthand what could happen when

Cashman's kettle boiled over. In 1974, during his first training camp with the Bruins, Milbury was doing his best to make an impression. During one drill, the defenseman repeatedly crossed paths with Cashman. The veteran promptly let Milbury know he was no longer playing college hockey.

"The puck kept coming off the wall because they were rimming it to the same side," Milbury said. "We kept bumping into each other and got into a stick fight. He bangs me over the shoulder. I bang him over the shoulder. I'm in control but not quite on the edge. Then he turned his stick over. Once he turned his stick over, I'm like, 'Shit, the chips just got a little heavier.' Fortunately, it got broken up."

By then, the 29-year-old Cashman was in his prime. He was coming off a year in 1973–74 when he reached career highs in every category: goals (30), assists (59), points (89), and penalty minutes (111). Cashman had become a do-it-all forward who was feared in every category of the game. He was the top-line grinder alongside Phil Esposito and Ken Hodge, tasked to do the dirty work to hunt down the puck for his linemates.

"His game is in the corners," Bobby Orr, Cashman's teammate in Boston and Oshawa, told the *Boston Globe*. "He's a tough guy. You have to be tough and aggressive to play in the corners. And if you play in the corners, you get into scrapes. He can handle himself. He's not vicious. He's not the kind of guy who's out on the ice to cut up somebody. If I had a team I'd like a lot of Wayne Cashmans on it."

When things got rough, Cashman was among the first to say goodbye to his gloves. Cashman had the resume—a pair of rings from 1970 and 1972—to back up his actions. During the first championship season, Cashman scored nine goals and 26 assists in 70 games. In 14 postseason games, Cashman complemented his nine points with 50 penalty minutes, second most on the team after Derek Sanderson (72).

By 1972, Cashman's game had taken off. The top-line left wing scored 23 goals and 29 assists in 74 games, all while recording 103 penalty minutes. Not many opponents were willing to get in Cashman's way once he hit cruising speed.

"He's really one of the best wings ever to play the game," Gerry Cheevers told *Sports Illustrated*. "At the Team Canada training camp last summer we were picking our all-time NHL team, and I insisted that we had to have Cashman as one of the five left wings. OK, he doesn't have the flair of a Bobby Hull, but championships aren't won only by the flashy guys. They're won in the corners and along the boards, and Cashman is the best of our era when it comes to playing in the corners and along the boards."

What Cashman didn't know at the time was that the Big Bad Bruins era was coming to an end. Esposito, his center, would not be his teammate for much longer. Orr's knees were wasting away with every shift. The Bruins needed players to help them transition from one generation to the next. Cashman would be the bridge.

On November 7, 1975, general manager Harry Sinden traded Esposito to the Rangers in one of the NHL's biggest blockbuster deals. Cashman did not take it well. He was Esposito's good friend as well as linemate. When Esposito told Cashman that Sinden had promised never to trade him, his winger believed it. But as upset as Cashman was about the trade, it was his job to welcome Brad Park and Jean Ratelle to the Bruins.

"I give credit to players like Cashman," Sinden said. "Park was a hated player on the Rangers. Ratelle, not so much. It's pretty hard to hate Jean Ratelle. But our players did not like the Rangers at all. There was a hate there. Not a hate like with Philadelphia, but there was a hate there. I was wondering how they were going to accept these players. Cashman was very upset. He was close to Phil. But they got over it and handled it beautifully. They could have turned on me."

Cashman and Ratelle became linemates. By 1977, Johnny Bucyk's final NHL season, there was only one choice to serve as captain: Cashman, Chief's Cup-winning teammate. Cashman had the presence and the accomplishments necessary to lead the room and carry out coach Don Cherry's marching orders of outworking and outmuscling opponents. The Big Bad Bruins had transformed into the Lunchpail AC, with Cashman leading the way for Milbury, Terry O'Reilly, Stan Jonathan, and John Wensink. By then, Cashman had become a toned-down version of the scrapper that once fought his way through the league. The older and wiser Cashman led in other ways. He set the example that his younger teammates followed.

The Bruins had some players who shone with greater brilliance than Cashman, such as Orr and Esposito. But they moved on from Boston. Cashman played in 1,027 career games, all in Black and Gold. By the time Cashman retired in 1983, Ray Bourque was a fourth-year pro. Cashman must have been doing a lot of things right to have survived for so long.

26

AN ABRUPT ENDING

On September 26, 1995, Normand Leveille took one final skate at Boston Garden before the old barn closed down for good. Had better luck been with Leveille, he might have been in uniform that night in the Bruins' preseason game against the Canadiens, wearing No. 19. Leveille, 32 years old at the time of the Garden's closing, certainly had the skill and pedigree to be a long-time NHLer.

Instead, the former first-round pick in 1981 needed the assistance of former teammate and fellow Montreal native Ray Bourque to skate around the Garden ice one final time.

It wasn't meant to be this way for Leveille. He was neither the biggest nor strongest forward playing junior hockey for Chicoutimi. But his skill, speed, and shot were enough to put him on the Bruins' radar. In his draft year, the clever Leveille scored 55 goals and 46 assists in 72 games. Two years earlier, the Bruins hit the jackpot when they drafted Bourque with the No. 8 pick. In 1981, they thought they had acquired a similar prodigy in Leveille, drafted 14th overall.

Under normal circumstances, the Bruins would have drafted Leveille and returned him to junior that fall. The rough-and-tumble NHL was no place for 18-year-olds unless they were exceptional talents. Leveille quickly informed his new employer that he belonged in that category.

During training camp that fall, Leveille opened eyes with his skating and scoring touch. After a pair of rookie games against the Flyers, Leveille's production made the Bruins think about keeping the teenager around for the start of the season. While his 5'10", 175-pound frame made him vulnerable to physical punishment, Leveille read opponents' intentions so well that he could slip around dangerous body checks and take the puck to the net.

"They were the kind of goals that if he scored them in Boston Garden, he would have taken all of the fans right out of their seats and had them cheering," Harry Sinden told the *Boston Globe*. "From what I've seen of him so far, I think Leveille is the best forward this team has drafted in a long, long time. He is both quick and fast. He skates like a Russian. If he keeps coming along the way I feel he

CAREERS DERAILED

The Bruins had high hopes for Gord Kluzak. When they made Kluzak the first overall pick in 1982, the 18-year-old had come off the defenseman assembly line: 6'4", 210 pounds, mobile, physical. In his draft year, Kluzak scored nine goals and 24 assists along with 110 penalty minutes in 38 games. Kluzak had no trouble transitioning from junior to the NHL in 1982–83, dressing for 70 games. Knee injuries, however, limited Kluzak to just 229 more games before he had to call it quits on November 12, 1990. He was only 26 years old.

Sixteen years after they drafted Kluzak, the Bruins picked Jonathan Girard, another promising defenseman, in the second round of the 1998 Draft. The right-shot Girard was an offensive-minded puck-moving defenseman. By 2002–03, Girard had developed into a slick and steady player who scored six goals and 16 assists in 73 games. He never played another NHL game. On July 24, 2003, Girard was in a car accident that left him with injuries serious enough to cut his NHL career short.

can, I think he can play for our team and make a contribution. This team needs what this kid has. I mean by that, the type of speed and quickness he shows."

As a rookie, Leveille scored 14 goals and 19 assists in 66 games. It was a very good start for the young wing. With Leveille up front and Bourque on the back end, the Bruins looked like they would have two promising French-Canadian talents in Boston for a long time. The projection among NHL personnel was Yvon Cournoyer, the Hall of Fame Canadien.

Leveille started his second NHL season at a point-per-game pace. But his ninth game would be his last. On October 23, 1982, Leveille played in the Bruins' 3–2 loss to the Canucks at Vancouver's Pacific Coliseum. He took a heavy hit from Marc Crawford and banged his head into the boards.

The damage from Crawford's hit, however, had nothing to do with the maelstrom that was already taking place within Leveille's head. Doctors would later discover that Leveille was born with an arteriovenous malformation—a tangle of blood vessels in his brain. Something as harmless as a sneeze could have triggered the tangle to let go.

After the first period, Leveille returned to the dressing room and complained of dizziness. By then, his life was already beginning to change because of a cerebral hemorrhage. He collapsed and was rushed to Vancouver General Hospital. Dr. Barry Woodhurst led an operation to save Leveille's life. The procedure halted the bleeding and relieved pressure in Leveille's brain.

In one way, Leveille was lucky. Medical personnel at the arena immediately identified he was in trouble and rushed him to Vancouver General. Had his episode taken place elsewhere—at home or in a hotel—he might not have made it to a hospital so quickly. Also, Leveille was in outstanding condition. Had he been weaker, he might not have survived the initial trauma.

But the incident turned Leveille's life upside down. After two weeks, he was taken off a ventilator. He was stricken with pleurisy. More than a month following his cerebral hemorrhage, Leveille was flown to Montreal, where he was admitted to the Montreal Neurological Institute to start his rehabilitation. He was paralyzed on his right side. His speech was affected.

"It was difficult," Bourque told the *Boston Globe* after visiting his former teammate in Montreal. "But it wasn't as hard as I expected it would be, seeing him. He looks pretty good. He recognized us, but we didn't stay long because you don't know what to say to him. I spoke to him in French and I'm sure he knew me."

On February 11, 1984, Leveille returned to Boston Garden for the first time since his illness. Eleven years later, Leveille came back to the Garden to close out the building's existence.

Leveille progressed miraculously, considering the gravity of his condition. He launched the Centre Normand Leveille, a camp in Drummondville, Quebec, for handicapped children. He speaks well in French, although he tires late in the day. He plays golf.

Life became pretty good for Leveille, considering his situation. But there could have been so much more to his life and career. Had he been healthy, Leveille could have become one of the best players of his generation.

27

HARRY

Harry Sinden was at the top of his profession. The 38-year-old coach of the Bruins had led his team to the championship, the organization's first Stanley Cup in 29 years. His charges included 22-year-old Bobby Orr, who, at his age, was primed to chase multiple Cups as he approached the sweet spot of his career. Sinden was embraced by a city that had become bewitched by the flair and the success of the high-flying Bruins.

But at the height of his powers, Sinden left both the bench and the game.

By Sinden's recollection, he won the Cup while earning $17,000. The league standard for his peers was approximately $30,000. Sinden asked for $25,000 after winning the Cup. Via general manager Milt Schmidt, owner Weston Adams declined to meet Sinden's price.

Sinden learned he could make $40,000 annually. However, he would have to leave hockey to do so. David Stirling, one of Sinden's acquaintances, hired the coach to serve as vice president of sales for Stirling Homex, a housing company in Rochester, New York. As much as the salary

exceeded expectations, leaving the Bruins was not what he wanted to do.

"I left for two years in tears," said Sinden.

Hockey, after all, was not just a profession for Sinden. Although he never played in the NHL, Sinden was a good amateur defenseman. He struck silver for Team Canada in the 1960 Olympics. A meeting with former Bruins GM Lynn Patrick led to a job offer as a player-coach for Kingston of the Eastern Professional Hockey League. As much as Sinden struggled with the game as a player, thinking about it and coaching it came easily.

In 1966, Sinden got his chance when he took over in Boston for Schmidt. They had finished in fifth place the year before after five straight sixth-place finishes.

"They had been in the cellar through the '60s," Sinden said. "The year before, they finally got to fifth place. When I got there, I took them back to sixth."

But the pieces were in place for Sinden. His first year behind the bench coincided with Orr's rookie season. Sinden had no doubt about Orr's future. The defenseman just needed more time and more help. Reinforcements arrived on May 15, 1967, when the Bruins acquired Phil Esposito, Ken Hodge, and Fred Stanfield from Chicago for Gilles Marotte, Pit Martin, and Jack Norris. Esposito, Orr, and the goaltending tandem of Gerry Cheevers and Ed Johnston gave Sinden the armaments he needed up the middle. By 1970, his players had ripened to run through the Rangers, Blackhawks, and Blues to win the Cup.

In that context, it is no wonder that Sinden, out of hockey and grinding in Rochester, regularly found himself in Buffalo at Sabres games, still thinking about the sport he loved. By the summer of 1972, Sinden and his coworkers were out of luck. Stirling Homex filed for bankruptcy.

WORST DRAFT PICKS

In 1994, 23 of the 26 players selected in the first round played at least one NHL game. Evgeni Ryabchikov was not one of them. With Harry Sinden at the helm, the Bruins swung and missed on Ryabchikov with the 21st pick, the third goalie drafted that year after Jamie Storr (No. 7) and Eric Fichaud (No. 16). Ryabchikov bounced between the AHL, ECHL, and WPHL before calling it quits on his North American career.

Like every other team, the Bruins have missed on others: Zach Hamill (first round, 2007), Lars Jonsson (first round, 2000), Johnathan Aitken (first round, 1996), Dave Pasin (first round, 1984), and Don Larway (first round, 1974).

But Sinden's unemployment in hockey turned out to be a blessing. By the summer of 1972, Team Canada was looking for a coach and GM for the upcoming Summit Series. Sinden got the job, partly because he didn't have any attachments to an NHL team.

The Summit Series wasn't just a hockey tournament. By its conclusion, it had become an important marker in Canadian history, international relations, and the Cold War. In the eighth and final game, Esposito scored two goals and two assists, while Paul Henderson netted the winner with 34 seconds remaining in the game.

"That's one of the great memories," Sinden said of his Summit Series experience. "One of the players, Serge Savard, he won five or six Cups. To this day, he says that stands out in his memory as much as any of those. Many players felt the same way. It had a political significance. The Cold War was going on and we were in the middle of it. A lot of people interpreted it as some kind of victory other than hockey. So it had a real significance to the psyche of the country."

Canada's success also helped Sinden get back into the NHL. On October 5, 1972, Sinden was hired as the fifth GM in Bruins history. Sinden's return coincided with the emergence of the World Hockey Association. The WHA claimed Cheevers, John McKenzie, and Derek Sanderson, three critical pieces of the Cup teams of 1970 and 1972. Dependable forward Ed Westfall went to the Islanders in expansion after 1972. Sinden would have to be active as a GM to keep the Bruins atop the league.

"The team was not going to stay together," Sinden said. "It had to be rebuilt."

By then, Sinden and the Bruins knew that it was just a matter of time before Orr's knees would limit the defenseman's brilliance. In 1972–73, Terry O'Reilly played his rookie season and became one of Sinden's primary building blocks. The following season, Sinden acquired Gilles Gilbert to serve as his go-to goalie before he signed with the WHA. On November 7, 1975, Sinden made perhaps his most significant transaction when he traded Esposito and Carol Vadnais to the Rangers for Brad Park, Jean Ratelle, and Joe Zanussi. Sinden recognized that Esposito's best goal-scoring games were behind him. In Park, Sinden projected he could form one of the most dynamic power-play duos in the game alongside Orr.

The hard-nosed teams of the mid-1970s advanced to the final three times: 1974 against Philadelphia, 1977 against Montreal, and 1978 against the Canadiens once more. The Bruins lost all three times. The Bruins recharged in 1979 after drafting Ray Bourque eighth overall, continuing their legacy of difference-making defensemen in the likes of Orr and Park.

Sinden would never win a Cup as GM. But he was recognized as one of the game's great builders when he entered the Hockey Hall of Fame in 1983. On October 17, 1995, when the Bruins beat the Blues by a 7–4 score, Sinden became the first GM in league history to win 1,000 games. He advanced to the final five times and built rosters that qualified for the playoffs in 29 straight seasons, a league record. The streak ended in 1997. He was replaced as GM by Mike O'Connell on November 1, 2000. Sinden served as president until August 9, 2006. He has since acted as senior adviser to owner Jeremy Jacobs.

28

COACHING TO A CUP

Claude Julien was in a bind. His team was down two games to the Canadiens, with the first round of the 2011 playoffs shifting onto enemy ice at Montreal's Bell Centre. The Bruins lost Game 2 at TD Garden by a 3–1 score, partly because of the absence of Zdeno Chara. The No. 1 defenseman participated in pregame warmups, but a virus left the captain dizzy, tired, and in no condition to take on his usual 25-minute-plus workload.

With five games remaining in which the Bruins had to win four times, Julien made one of the best decisions of his coaching career. Upon consultation with management and his assistant coaches, Julien decided to unite Chara and Dennis Seidenberg as his No. 1 defensive pairing.

Before then, Chara had been playing alongside Johnny Boychuk. Seidenberg was on the second pairing with Tomas Kaberle. It was not a move without risk. By putting Chara and Seidenberg together, Julien was risking a top-heavy defensive unit. But defense has always been Julien's strength.

As a player, Julien worked the blue line for 14 career NHL games, all for the Quebec Nordiques. The right-shot

Julien was a smart, physical, stay-at-home defenseman. But he did not have the wheels to become a permanent NHL blue liner. He worked the corners and the net-front real estate in the minors, where he learned to apply his thinking in the areas where his skating fell short.

Upon his retirement as a player, coaching seemed like a natural thing for Julien. He enjoyed processing the game, teaching it, and devising ways to beat opponents. He got his break when, after two years of being an assistant for Hull of the QMJHL, he became the head coach in 1996–97. It did not hurt that the Olympiques won the Memorial Cup in Julien's first season as the man in charge. In 2000, Hockey Canada chose Julien as its coach for the World Junior Championship. With future NHLers such as Jason Spezza, Jay Bouwmeester, Brad Richards, Dany Heatley, and Michael Ryder under his watch, Julien and the Canadians won bronze.

The NHL noticed Julien's results. Later that year, Edmonton hired Julien to serve as its AHL head coach in Hamilton. By 2002–03, Hamilton had a split affiliation with Edmonton and Montreal. The latter was in the market for a head coach after firing Michel Therrien. Julien, as a native French speaker, was the right man to replace Therrien.

Julien's stay in Montreal did not last as long as he hoped. In 2003–04, his first full season with the Canadiens, Julien beat his future team in the opening round of the playoffs. After falling behind 3–1 to the Bruins, Julien instructed his players to approach every game as its own entity rather than thinking about a bleak big picture. The Canadiens bought in to Julien's message and rallied for three straight wins against his future employer.

Even so, it was not enough to buy Julien another full season. On January 14, 2006, Julien was fired. That summer, he landed in New

Jersey, where management believed Julien was the right fit to lead its defense-first system.

It looked as if Julien was doing just that. As of April 2, 2007, the Devils were leading the Atlantic Division and preparing for the playoffs. But with three games remaining in the regular season, general manager Lou Lamoriello sacked Julien and took over as head coach. Julien's ouster came one day after his Devils beat the Bruins at Continental Airlines Arena 3–1. The Bruins, who were practicing in Montreal when Julien's firing became official, thought it was a late April Fool's Day joke.

Lamoriello's decision became one of the best gifts the Bruins would receive. The previous summer, new GM Peter Chiarelli had considered Julien as his choice to replace Mike Sullivan. The two Ottawa natives were familiar with each other. Chiarelli had admired Julien's ability to coach young players in Hull. But before Chiarelli could pitch Julien on the Bruins, he had already accepted New Jersey's offer.

Chiarelli was in a bind. He had signed Lewis to a four-year contract. The GM had said Lewis' job was safe despite a 13th-place finish. But Chiarelli believed that Julien's no-nonsense approach, commitment to structure, and defensive-minded philosophy would be good additions in Boston. Chiarelli fired Lewis on June 15, 2007. Six days later, Julien was named as Lewis' replacement.

The changes on defense became clear quickly. Under Lewis, the Bruins weren't sure what to do in terms of coverage or breakouts. There was no gray area with Julien. The Bruins were to play a box-and-one collapsing zone system. One defenseman would almost always be stationed in front of the net, where the best scoring chances usually took place. His partner would be free to engage the puck carrier down low. The center would be critical to supporting the defensemen. He would have to be deep in the defensive zone for coverage and available as a first outlet. He would also have to be aware to cover passing lanes to the point. The wingers would be responsible for challenging the points, but also to be quick to slam down in the slot to limit chances.

It took the Bruins time to adjust to the new system. In Julien's first season, Manny Fernandez, once expected to be the No. 1 goalie following a trade with Minnesota, was limited to only four appearances because of a knee injury. Defensemen Dennis Wideman, Aaron Ward, and Andrew Ference, who were acquired the year before, were still adapting to their new organization. Patrice

COACHING REBOOT

Peter Chiarelli said that hiring Claude Julien was the best move he made as Bruins GM. Chiarelli executed his shrewdest transaction to wipe out one of his most ill-advised decisions.

After declining to retain former coach Mike Sullivan, Chiarelli made the hire of Dave Lewis official on June 29, 2006. Lewis, the longtime assistant to Scotty Bowman in Detroit, took over the Red Wings bench following his boss' retirement in 2002. Lewis lasted just two seasons as the head coach in Detroit before he was replaced by Mike Babcock.

It was twice as long as Lewis' stay in Boston. The Bruins never gained traction under Lewis' guidance, stumbling to a 13th-place finish (35–41–6) in 2006–07. Thirty-eight skaters played for the Bruins that season along with five goalies. The team didn't play with much defensive structure. It was regularly called for too many men on the ice. Lewis did not allow first-year captain Zdeno Chara, one of the league's most intimidating players, to fight.

After just one season into a four-year contract, Lewis paid for the underwhelming results with his job. Lewis was fired on June 15, 2007. Six days later, Julien assumed Lewis' position.

Bergeron played in only 10 games before suffering a season-ending concussion.

But Julien's scrappy team finished in eighth place. They took the top-ranked Canadiens to seven games in the opening round of the playoffs before losing to the favorites. Zdeno Chara rebounded after a tough first season in Boston. They had promising young players in Milan Lucic and David Krejci. Above all else, Julien had a keeper in net in Tim Thomas.

Julien's system was a perfect fit for Thomas. By emphasizing the middle of the defensive zone, the Bruins left Thomas to take care of shots from the outside. He was good at that. As long as Thomas could handle the first shot, his defense was taught to take care of any rebounds.

By Julien's second season, the defensive foundation had taken place. With Thomas en route to the first of two Vezina Trophies, the Bruins finished 2008–09 as the stingiest team in the league (2.32 goals allowed per game). At the same time, they added offense to their game. Julien assembled a strong offensive line in Lucic, Marc Savard, and Phil Kessel. Bergeron, still recovering from his concussion, played a defensive role on the second line. Krejci centered an excellent third line between Blake Wheeler and Michael Ryder. The coach who had always been known for defense was in charge of the second-best offense in the league (3.29 goals scored per game). Julien won the Jack Adams Trophy as the NHL's top coach.

The Bruins, however, were upset in the second round by Carolina. A year later, Julien's job security weakened after a second-round exit to the Flyers after holding a 3–0 series lead. But Julien kept firm to his beliefs in 2010–11. He preached 60 minutes of engagement. He demanded defensive accountability. He didn't panic when the Bruins lost their first two games of the playoffs. He kept his players focused through three Game 7s against Montreal, Tampa Bay, and Vancouver. He was rewarded with his first Stanley Cup.

Julien's employment came under scrutiny again after the Bruins failed to make the playoffs in 2014–15. After Chiarelli was fired, Julien wondered whether he would be next, even though he knew what changes he had to make. That season, the Bruins' singular problem was their breakout. The team that had once regularly cleared pucks and transitioned into its rush game could not get out of its own end. Two-man forechecks hammered down on the defensemen and kept the Bruins pinned in their own zone. Even before Chiarelli's firing, Julien was busy thinking about how he'd adjust the breakout in 2015–16 to improve the team's 23rd-ranked offense.

Julien's idea was to get his defensemen going up the ice quicker. Instead of having both defensemen stay at home, he wanted one to activate, join the rush, and push the pace up the ice. In previous seasons, Julien wanted his forwards to fill the lanes, spread the ice, and advance together. In 2015–16, the forwards would be free to overload on one side of the ice and be in position to either receive short passes or get on the forecheck quickly to cause neutral-zone turnovers.

New GM Don Sweeney took his time. Sweeney and Julien spoke multiple times about the changes that had to take place. Julien convinced Sweeney that he was ready and willing to make adjustments. That Julien was about to start the first season of a multiyear extension did not hurt his cause. On June 5, 2015, 16 days into his tenure, Sweeney announced that Julien and assistants Doug Houda, Doug Jarvis, Joe Sacco, and Bob Essensa would be back.

By the start of 2015–16, Julien was the NHL's longest-tenured coach with his current team. The loaded roster he once had was diminished, with Lucic and Dougie Hamilton dealt to Los Angeles and Calgary during the offseason. Young defensemen such as Zach Trotman, Joe Morrow, and Colin Miller had to assume bigger roles. Their inexperience meant that the once-sturdy defense faded to the bottom third of the league. But Julien's adjustments had led to a top-three offense. Julien has never been afraid of change. Evolution has always been one of his strengths.

29

A LEGENDARY RALLY

The game and the season were over. With 14:31 remaining in regulation, Nazem Kadri had slammed home the rebound of a Phil Kessel shot to give the Maple Leafs a 4–1 Game 7 lead in the opening round of the 2013 playoffs. David Krejci hammered the puck back into his own net in frustration after Kadri's goal.

On the bench, Milan Lucic was thinking about the end, not just of the year but of an era. Lucic understood that a first-round exit could turn the organization upside down, from GM to coach to players. The Bruins, built for a Cup run, were instead on their way to being torn down.

"When you're looking at the clock wind down with half a period left at 4–1," Lucic said, "'you start thinking to yourself, 'Is this the end of the group here?' "

Nothing about the last two days had gone right for the Bruins. One night earlier, on May 12, 2013, the Bruins lost Game 6 on the road to the Leafs 2–1. During the game, the Bruins learned they would have to remain in Toronto overnight instead of flying back to Boston because

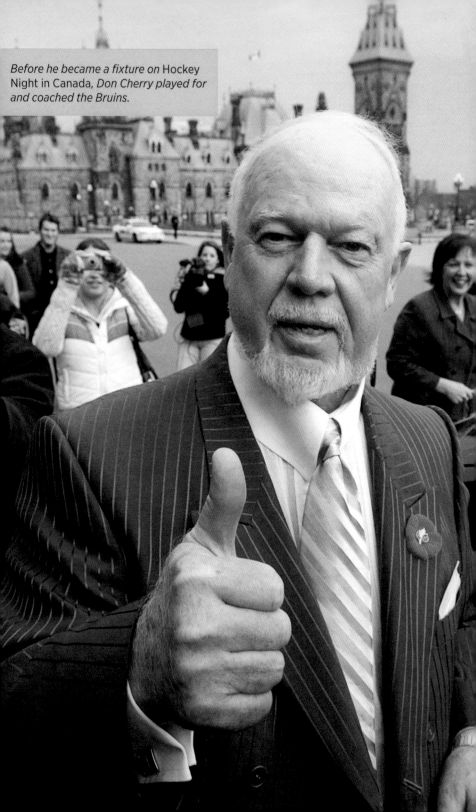

Before he became a fixture on Hockey Night in Canada, *Don Cherry played for and coached the Bruins.*

of a maintenance issue with their plane. While the Leafs traveled to Boston after their Game 6 win, the Bruins were stuck in Toronto, their usual routine scotched because of the malfunction.

The Bruins scored first in Game 7. But the Leafs rallied for four straight goals, including what looked like Kadri's finishing strike.

Lucic took it upon himself to make sure that system change would have to wait. Later in the third period, after taking a dish from Krejci, Lucic powered the puck down the left wing. Krejci followed his wingman, drawing three of the Leafs his way. By the time Lucic curled around the net and looked for support, the Leafs had been sucked in down low, leaving Nathan Horton open at the left circle. Lucic connected with Horton. The right wing buried his shot at 9:18 of the third. The Bruins were down two goals—still a significant deficit, but not an impossible one to overcome.

They would need an extra body to do so.

With approximately two minutes remaining in regulation, coach Claude Julien pulled Tuukka Rask. He sent out six of his best players: Lucic, Krejci, Horton, Patrice Bergeron, Jaromir Jagr, and Zdeno Chara. The six players knew where they had to be in the offensive zone. Chara would set up at the right point, ready to unload a one-timer. The right-shot Bergeron would be on the left point, also in one-timing position. Krejci would be on the left-side half-boards. Lucic would be the net-front presence, taking away James Reimer's sightlines. Horton would be in the high slot as a secondary screener, tipper, or shooter. Jagr would be off to the right side, hopefully getting lost in coverage.

The Bruins didn't panic. They had a job to do: pull within one.

Chara, from the point, slapped a puck on goal. Reimer kicked out the shot with his right pad. Krejci was in the right spot to settle the rebound and get it back up to Bergeron at the left point. With the Leafs packed in down low, Bergeron had plenty of time and space to consider his options. Bergeron read that his shooting lane was closed down. So he slid a cross-ice pass to Chara at the right point. Bergeron identified that Chara would have enough time to rip off a shot before the Leafs shifted his way.

Bergeron was right. Chara swung a one-timer on goal. Reimer stopped Chara's shot, but pushed the rebound back into the slot. Lucic, who had gained separation from Carl Gunnarsson, punched home the rebound to make it a 4–3 game. The Bruins had 82 seconds to tie the game.

They needed only 31. After Bergeron won the following faceoff against Jay McClement, the Bruins gained the offensive zone. This time, to alter Toronto's defense, they went into a different formation. Bergeron would be the lone point man. Krejci (left) and Jagr (right) would be the high-circle options. Horton remained in the high slot. Lucic would be the right-side goal-line man. Chara, the biggest man in the league, rotated down to be Reimer's eclipse.

After taking the puck from Krejci, Bergeron saw he had an opening. Chara was screening Reimer. Horton was in the high slot, his stick down on the ice to tip the puck. Nikolai Kulemin, the Toronto forward tasked to cover the point, was caught in no-man's land—not close enough to Bergeron to get a stick on the shot, and too far away from the slot to help out his teammates. With Chara occupying every inch of net-front real estate, Reimer never had a chance to see or stop Bergeron's shot. The score was 4–4 with 50.2 seconds remaining before overtime.

"I could have gone back to Krejci on the half-wall or go to Jags on the other half-wall," Bergeron told the *Boston Globe*. "They were both open there. But I had a good lane for a shot and I knew we had some good traffic with Z and even Horty in the slot."

TD Garden shook after Bergeron's game-tying goal. The arena continued to rumble after 60 minutes and the teams retreated to their dressing rooms. The Bruins were not prepared to let a three-goal rally turn into nothing in overtime.

The game-winning OT sequence started with Bergeron one-timing a puck on net. Reimer stopped Bergeron's shot. But Jake Gardiner, with Tyler Seguin hounding him for the puck, couldn't clear the rebound out of danger. Mikhail Grabovski swooped in to help, but the forward couldn't get the puck away either. Cody Franson found the puck and backhanded it out of the crease and what he thought would be up the left-side wall. Instead, Bergeron intercepted the clear and thundered the puck home at 6:05 of overtime for the winner.

No team had ever rallied from a three-goal deficit in Game 7 of the playoffs to live another day. The Bruins had made NHL history.

30

GRAPES

It may not be fair that Don Cherry is likely to be best remembered by Bruins fans as the coach who oversaw one of the most humiliating moments in team history, captured by three painful words: too many men.

It may not have been Cherry's fault that night on May 10, 1979, at the Montreal Forum. Don Marcotte, after all, had stayed on the ice for a long time as Guy Lafleur's shadow. The Bruins were caught up in the moment of leading Game 7 of the Stanley Cup semifinal 4–3 against rivals who always came out on top.

Yet as the coach, it was Cherry's responsibility to make sure that the right number of players was on the ice at all times. To the observers watching the game, it sure looked like referee Bob Myers and linesman John D'Amico gave Cherry and the Bruins plenty of leash with which to correct a mistake that would become fatal. But at 17:26 of the third period, D'Amico had no choice but to blow his whistle.

Of course, on the power play, Lafleur scored on Gilles Gilbert to tie the game 4–4 with 74 seconds remaining in regulation. And of course, in overtime, Yvon Lambert scored

to give the Canadiens the win and the series. Cherry was fired at season's end.

"The officiating gave us all the time in the world to get the guy off the ice, which we weren't able to do," said Harry Sinden. "As I understand it—I was in the stands—we were trying to keep Marcotte on Lafleur. It became a mixup on the bench. Lafleur was on, off, then came back out. Two people jumped over, including Marcotte. After the game, Cherry said no player was to blame. He was to blame. I agreed with him. Now, he's not really to blame, but if you watch coaches in those last minutes of play when you're in that kind of player movement and changes, coaches sometimes get a hold of the player's scruff of the neck. They shove them out or hold them back. They're watching the change. We didn't make a good change. It was probably two players got mixed up more than Don's fault. It was too bad, because they scored on the penalty and we ended up losing."

But Cherry, who would become larger than life on *Hockey Night in Canada*, did a whole lot more in Boston than end up on the wrong end of a year-ending penalty. Cherry's commanding presence behind the Bruins bench helped give the organization a swagger and confidence that tapped into the Black-and-Gold DNA.

"There were a lot of influences in that room," said Mike Milbury. "None more than Grapes."

Cherry played just one NHL game as a player. That came in 1955 with the Bruins. The results that eluded Cherry as a player, however, took place behind the bench. He served his AHL apprenticeship with the Rochester Braves for three seasons. He then got his chance up top.

The Bruins hired Cherry in 1974 to replace Bep Guidolin. They wanted the no-nonsense Cherry to grab a hold of the room and help steer the team back to its 1970 and 1972 heights. The Bruins didn't know it at the time, but their glory days were over. It would be up

FROM THE ICE TO THE PRESS BOX

Don Cherry is a Canadian icon, not because of his career as a player or coach. Cherry has become one of the sport's most famous people because of his television role on *Hockey Night in Canada*—specifically Coach's Corner, the segment where he banters about hockey with help from longtime straight man Ron MacLean.

Cherry is not alone among ex-Bruins who have progressed to television and radio. In Boston, former Bruins teammates Andy Brickley and Bob Beers serve as the team's TV and radio analysts, respectively. They have company around the league. Other ex-Bruins who have moved upstairs to the press box: Nick Boynton (Arizona), Peter McNab (Colorado), Jason York (Montreal), Butch Goring (Islanders), Phil Esposito (Tampa Bay), and Shane Hnidy (Winnipeg).

Ex-Bruins with national media jobs include Garry Galley (Sportsnet), Mike Milbury (NBC), and Anson Carter (NBC).

to Cherry to help them transition from the Big Bad Bruins to the Lunchpail AC.

In 400 games, Cherry's teams won 231 times. He is the fourth-winningest coach in team history. He oversaw the last days of Bobby Orr, Phil Esposito, and Johnny Bucyk. When Sinden traded Esposito and Carol Vadnais to the Rangers in the 1975 blockbuster, Cherry broke the news to the star center, then made sure the team didn't turn against the GM. Under Cherry, Terry O'Reilly, Peter McNab, Jean Ratelle, Brad Park, and Milbury rose to prominence.

As a coach, Cherry didn't complicate the game. He instructed his players to keep a third man high in the offensive zone. If a defenseman pinched down the wall to keep the cycle alive, Cherry wanted his forward back to cover up. In the defensive zone, if a defenseman got in trouble under pressure, Cherry instructed him to go up or around the wall and out, not through the middle of the ice.

While Xs and Os weren't necessarily Cherry's thing, tapping into his players' emotions was his sweet spot. Cherry inspired the Bruins to go through opponents and do everything possible to win. When they did what he wanted, Cherry had their backs.

"He owned the room," Milbury said. "No doubt."

It's probably not a coincidence that Milbury took to coaching upon retirement because of Cherry's inspiration. They both lived north of Boston. Cherry insisted that they drive to practice together. Milbury agreed, knowing that saying no to his coach was not an option. On their drives, they noticed something that would become legendary in both of their lives.

During their commute on Route 1, Cherry and Milbury spotted a weed growing in the median between a set of old iron rails. Even in the middle of winter, whenever they drove by, the weed was still there. Cherry dubbed it a Bruin type of weed—tough and resilient.

One spring day, they saw a cleaning crew working in the median. Cherry was terrified that they'd yank out the weed.

"Mike, you've got to get the weed!" Cherry told Milbury.

Cherry stopped his car. Again, acknowledging it was impossible to question his coach, Milbury got out.

"He stops on the side of the stupid highway, right by the Tobin Bridge, and I've got to go get the weed," Milbury recalled. "I'm dodging 60 mph traffic to get to the median strip. I'm trying to pull out the weed by its roots. We get it and drive to a gas station. He gets a newspaper, wraps the weed up, wets it, and takes it home to plant it in the garden."

Some time later, Milbury asked Cherry how the weed was doing. Cherry admitted that Rose, his wife, had thrown out the weed while cleaning the garden. Milbury, however, had learned the lesson. That he never forgot it was a credit to his coach.

31

PERFECT ENDING—ELSEWHERE

or 11 seasons, Ray Bourque and Patrick Roy did battle as Bruin and Canadien. The French-Canadian superstars competed fiercely on the ice. But during the off-season, as members at the same golf club in Montreal, Bourque and Roy became friends. Sometimes, they good-naturedly discussed life as possible teammates.

"I always told him he was going to have to come play in Boston," Bourque said. "He said, 'Oh no, you've got to play in Montreal.'"

Neither scenario happened. On March 6, 2000, the two rivals became teammates, but in Denver, not Boston or Montreal.

By then, Bourque had been a Bruin for almost 21 full seasons. Neither Bourque nor the organization had any intentions of putting him in colors other than Black and Gold. But that year, the Bruins were on pace to miss the playoffs for the second time in four seasons. Goalies Byron Dafoe, Robb Tallas, and John Grahame were under regular assault from opposing shooters. Joe Thornton, considered the player of the future, had yet to develop into a franchise center.

The Bruins were in the middle of controversy regarding Marty McSorley. On February 21, the former Edmonton tough guy swung his stick at Donald Brashear and tagged the Vancouver heavyweight on the head. McSorley was suspended by the league for the rest of the season and was charged with assault.

All this wore on Bourque. For all his accomplishments, he had never won a Cup. Bourque and the Bruins fell short in the final in 1988 and 1990, both times against the Oilers. The vacancy in his trophy case wasn't just troubling Bourque. It was reflecting in his play.

"The atmosphere wasn't good," Bourque told *Sports Illustrated*. "I needed to get out for my own head. I wasn't as consistent, wasn't as sharp. That was mental. To get the best out of myself, I needed a different environment. If I had stayed in Boston, I wouldn't have played next year. I would've called it quits."

So Bourque did what he never expected to do. On February 28, he approached general manager Harry Sinden and requested a trade. Bourque didn't want to leave Boston. But he wanted to chase a Cup and re-energize a game that had faded because of the Bruins' struggles. Sinden told Bourque he would see what he could do. On March 4, after a 3–0 loss at home to the Flyers, Bourque grabbed the puck as a keepsake.

Sinden respected Bourque like few other players. The GM had regularly made Bourque his highest-paid player and refused to go above the defenseman's salary threshold for any of his teammates. Sinden had watched Bourque grow from a shy 18-year-old into the organization's best all-around defenseman.

Sinden was not afraid of moving big-name players. He had done so in 1975 when he traded future Hall of Fame Player and two-time ring winner Phil Esposito to the Rangers. But trading Bourque felt different to Sinden. The GM's priority was to improve his team by trading the franchise defenseman. But he also acknowledged Bourque's wish for a Cup. He wanted to do his captain right.

By that point of the season, Bourque's destinations were limited. The Bruins would not be able to maximize their return for the 39-year-old defenseman.

At the same time, Bourque's preference was to stay in the Eastern Conference. Philadelphia was an intriguing option. The Flyers were a good team, with Mark Recchi, John LeClair, and Eric Lindros leading the charge. GM Bobby Clarke was interested in upgrading his defense to support goalies John Vanbiesbrouck and Brian Boucher. Wayne Cashman, Bourque's former teammate, was an assistant coach to Roger Neilson. Bourque would have helped the Flyers make a run.

But when Sinden and assistant GM Mike O'Connell surveyed the return for Bourque, the Flyers' response did not compare to Colorado's. The Avalanche were the seventh-place team in the Western Conference. They wanted Bourque's blue-line services badly. It showed in GM Pierre Lacroix's offer.

After the Bruins bundled big wing Dave Andreychuk into the deal, Colorado's response was the following: veteran Brian Rolston, promising center Samuel Pahlsson, intimidating defensive prospect Martin Grenier, and a 2000 first-round pick. The return satisfied Sinden. Bourque wasn't so sure.

Bourque thought Sinden would trade him to an Eastern team. He was surprised when he heard that Colorado would be his destination. After processing the trade, Bourque acknowledged the Avalanche would be a good fit. He'd be playing in front of Roy, his good buddy. He was an Olympic teammate of Joe Sakic and Adam Foote. The Avalanche had two ex-Bruins in Dave Reid and Jeff Odgers. Up front, Colorado had masses of talent in Sakic, Peter Forsberg, Chris Drury, and Milan Hejduk.

Upon his arrival, Bourque finished out the regular season with 14 points in 14 games. But it wasn't meant to be in the playoffs for the Avalanche. Bourque scored one goal and eight assists in 13 games, not enough to help his new team advance past the Western Conference Final.

The Avalanche reloaded the following season. Sakic led the way with 54 goals and 64 assists in 82 games. Bourque scored seven goals and 52 assists in 80 games. Lacroix traded for heavyweight Kings defenseman Rob Blake for the playoff push. Bourque's message to himself and his teammates that spring was Mission 16W: 16 wins and the Cup would be his.

Bourque and the Avalanche completed their mission after besting the Devils in the final. After Sakic accepted the Cup from commissioner Gary Bettman, he swiftly handed off the trophy to Bourque. Finally, in the last game of his career, the Cup was his. He wanted to share it with Bruins fans.

On June 13, Bourque brought the Cup to Boston for a celebration at City Hall Plaza. It seemed strange for Bostonians to cheer for a player who had won a championship for another team. But Bourque wasn't just any player.

32

EMBRACING AN ENEMY

Brad Park did not like the Bruins. As a member of the Rangers, Park traded shots with the Bruins for his first two pro seasons. In 1969–70, Park and the Rangers did battle with the Bruins in the opening round of the playoffs and came up short.

On the ice, Park made his displeasure with his opponents known, with both his stick and his fists. But it was another thing when Park made his comments part of the public record in *Play the Man*, his 1971 book he cowrote with Stan Fischler. Park did not pull his punches when discussing the hated Bruins.

On Bobby Orr: "Another myth about Orr is that he is a gentlemanly and a clean player. Actually Orr can be a hatchet man just like some of his Boston teammates. It bugs me to see him do that because he doesn't have to revert to the cheap stuff in order to succeed."

On Derek Sanderson: "A flake."

On John McKenzie: "A guy who hits people from behind and then runs away."

On Phil Esposito: "About Esposito, he's an extraordinary stick handler and superb shooter, but he doesn't have

any guts. He's carried in that department by the animals on the Boston team. Esposito runs people from behind."

Park's comments did not win him any friends in the Boston dressing room. In the 1972 final, the Bruins had no reservations about making Park their preferred target. After Gerry Cheevers shut out the Rangers in Game 6 and ended the Rangers' season, Park had no intentions of entering the handshake line until he saw Orr, the only defenseman better than him in the league, waiting to greet his rivals.

So it was a shock to both Park and the Bruins when he and Jean Ratelle became, on November 7, 1975, the latest Black-and-Gold members—for Esposito, no less. Harry Sinden had traded a legend to New York. Sinden brought back a defenseman the Bruins once despised.

Park was in Oakland on a road trip when he got the news. He knew something was up when Rangers coach Ron Stewart called Park that morning and instructed him to come to his hotel room. By then, Park knew he had been traded. He just didn't know his destination. Park could not believe when Stewart told him that GM Emile Francis had wheeled him to Boston. This was the city where Park required FBI protection at Boston Garden because of threats he received upon publication of his book.

"I was very upset at first by the trade," Park recalled to *Hockey Pictorial-World* in 1977. "It was a terrible shock. I had 'New York Ranger' tattooed on my heart. Even now I find myself writing 'New York Ranger' after my name on autographs and have to scribble it out. I had no inkling I'd be traded, none at all. In fact, I never thought I would be. The Cat once told me he'd never trade me. I really thought I'd be there until I was 35 or 40, you know—until I either retired or something."

Park had given Sinden plenty of data as an opponent. But in 1972, shortly after the Bruins won their second Cup in three seasons, Sinden got to know Park as one of his own. Park was part of the Canadian roster that Sinden coached during the eight-game Summit Series against the Soviet Union. As much as Sinden understood how good Park was while watching him for the Rangers, he developed a greater appreciation for his talent while coaching him in the international, Cold War spotlight. Park could do just about everything—skate like a whirlwind, rush the puck, run the power play, kill penalties, and fight anybody who was willing to take him on.

Three years later, Sinden knew his roster needed an upgrade. The Bruins started 1975–76 poorly. Orr was approaching the end. So Sinden targeted the 27-year-old Park, figuring that having the

RIVALS JOIN THE BRUINS

Chris Nilan is Boston through and through. He grew up in West Roxbury, a Boston neighborhood. He attended Catholic Memorial High School and Northeastern University. But for eight seasons, Nilan considered the Bruins his enemies. That's what happens when you play for the Canadiens, regardless of your upbringing. Knuckles became a Montreal legend because of his hard-charging style and willingness to drop the mitts against anybody, including the Bruins.

So it was odd for Nilan, who had moved on to the Rangers, to join his hometown team when he was traded for Greg Johnston and cash on June 28, 2000. Nilan played for the Bruins for parts of two seasons before he returned to Montreal on waivers.

Other disliked opponents who joined the Bruins: Guy Lapointe (Montreal), Kevin Stevens (Pittsburgh), Rogie Vachon (Montreal, Los Angeles, Detroit), Brian Leetch (Rangers), and Steve Begin (Montreal).

league's top two blue liners would not be a bad thing. They did not play together at even strength. But Orr and Park worked the point on the power play, moving pucks up to Ratelle, Johnny Bucyk, and Wayne Cashman, which was a wondrous thing to Sinden's eyes.

"Absolutely terrific. The greatest blue line on the power play ever put together," Sinden said of the 10 games they played together before knee surgery ended Orr's season. "They both played the right side, which became a bit of a problem on the power play. But both were dynamite from there. Brad Park was the greatest shooter of a rolling puck. Brad Park could shoot a rolling puck better than anybody. Players have to settle it down. He wouldn't. He could take the puck off the boards that was rolling and shoot it. It was going to be great. They sure got a lot of shots."

Upon meeting his new teammates in Vancouver for the first time after the trade, it was Orr who led the handshakes to greet Park. The Bruins accepted the player they formerly loathed.

By 1976–77, the blue line became Park's. Orr had moved on to Chicago. Coach Don Cherry, however, didn't want Park to attempt to mimic Orr's skill set. Cherry believed Park would serve his team better by focusing on defense first instead of rushing the puck and cheating up the ice at every opportunity. That year, Park scored 12 goals and 55 assists for 67 points. Park's play helped the Bruins advance to the final, where they lost to the Canadiens in four games. It was the first of three straight postseason setbacks the Bruins suffered against Montreal.

The following season, Park turned in arguably his best performance, scoring 22 goals and 57 assists in 80 games. But for the sixth and final time in his career, Park finished second in Norris Trophy voting as the league's best all-around defenseman. Where he was No. 2 to Orr on the five previous occasions, this time Park was second to Larry Robinson. The Montreal defenseman also had the last laugh in the playoffs, when the Canadiens beat the Bruins in the final in seven games. That postseason, Park scored nine goals, tying Orr's record for most playoff strikes in one year.

Park and the Bruins completed the Montreal hat trick in 1978–79, this time with too many men.

"What more could we have possibly done to win it? That's what hurts," Park told the *Toronto Star*. "We played great hockey and pushed them to the absolute limit. We'll look back it and think of a dozen little things that could have turned it our way. Give the Canadiens and especially Guy Lafleur credit. They just didn't quit, especially when we had that 3–1 lead in the third period."

Bad knees continued to wear Park down. He played his last season in Boston in 1982–83 before playing for Detroit for two more years.

33

DEFENSIVE DEPENDABILITY

Lionel Hitchman had a hard job. For eight seasons, he was the defensive wingman to Eddie Shore. Not many players could have fulfilled this position. Shore was a wildcard, always at risk of boiling over and doing damage both to opponents and to the Bruins because of his temper. It often fell to Hitchman, Shore's partner, to stabilize the pairing and the team. When Shore went up the ice on one of his signature romps with the puck, Hitchman hung back to stave off counterattacks. If Shore erupted, Hitchman was there to help defuse the fireworks.

It is no wonder the Bruins made Hitchman their second captain in team history. From 1927 to 1931, Hitchman served as the Bruins' leader in his quiet and dependable manner. Points were not his concern. Stout defense and wins were his pursuit. In 1929, Hitchman helped lead the Bruins to their first Stanley Cup. Opponents could not do much against the steady defending of the 6'1" Hitchman, a master of good positioning, a sound stick, and physical play.

Hitchman had just one assist in five playoff games against the Canadiens and Rangers. But the pairing of Hitchman and Shore allowed the Bruins

to beat Montreal three straight times, then take two games over the Rangers to win their first title. The Bruins scored nine goals in the five games. At the other end, Hitchman and Shore defended so well that Tiny Thompson kept his net free of all but three pucks in the five wins over the Canadiens and the Rangers.

It wasn't always this way before Hitchman's arrival. In 1924–25, the organization's inaugural season, the Bruins won only six of their 30 games. It was a poor team missing talent. Hitchman would become one of the significant additions in the young organization's turnaround.

Hitchman, a Toronto native, had moved to Ottawa and was playing for the Senators. One of Hitchman's teammates was King Clancy, who would go on to do big things with the Maple Leafs. Clancy was Ottawa's best defenseman. Hitchman did not see much action. The Bruins needed help on defense, and Hitchman was one of their targets.

The Senators considered a loan of Hitchman to Boston, where he would get more playing time. At first, the Bruins did not think much of Ottawa's pity.

"I cannot accept charity from the Ottawa club or any other club for that matter, and furthermore I do not intend to," owner Charles Adams told the *Montreal Gazette*. "I appreciate [manager Tommy] Gorman's offer but we would a great deal rather lose with our own men than win with players borrowed from other clubs. We will stand or fall upon merits of the team of our own that we can put on the ice…I am ready to buy hockey players, or trade them but I haven't got to where I have any desire to borrow them."

Adams and the Senators settled on a more agreeable financial transaction. The Bruins purchased Hitchman's services from the Senators midway through the 1924–25 season. In 1925–26, his first full season as a Bruin, Hitchman became teammates with an

ON THIS DATE

FEBRUARY 22, 1934

Lionel Hitchman plays the final game of his career. It is against Ottawa, his former team. The Senators beat the Bruins 3-1.

ex-nemesis: Sprague Cleghorn. Two years earlier, while Hitchman was in Ottawa and Cleghorn was in Montreal, the two had clashed in the playoffs. Cleghorn cross-checked Hitchman in the face, a foul so violent that the Canadiens took the unusual measure of suspending their own player.

Hitchman and Cleghorn got over their previous disagreements and became good teammates. One year later, Hitchman got an even better teammate when Shore became a Bruin. The left-shot, stay-at-home Hitchman was the perfect partner for the right-shot, swashbuckling Shore.

"Hitchman was usually paired with Eddie Shore after Shore joined the team in 1926–27," wrote Eric Zweig in *Art Ross: The Hockey Legend Who Built the Bruins*, "and it was often said that it was Hitchman's defensive prowess that allowed Shore to become an offensive force."

Hitchman, however, was on the wrong end of Shore's actions late in the 1929 championship season. On March 1, during a game against Ottawa, his former team, Hitchman suffered a broken jaw. Shore, attempting to clear the zone, sent the puck into his partner's face. Hitchman completed the game, but wore a helmet after the injury. He became one of the first players in league history to wear a helmet.

The injury took away from Hitchman's game. By the conclusion of 1931, when Hitchman failed to score a goal, reporters in Montreal were wondering whether the defenseman would be sold to the Canadiens. Adams put an end to any such whispers.

"At no time have I considered the sale or transfer of captain Lionel Hitchman, and I cannot understand from what source such an unfounded rumor has circulated," Adams told the *Boston Globe*. "Now that the season is over, Hitchman will undergo a very thorough examination in an effort to discover what has been his trouble. Undoubtedly it is physical. Dr. Arlie Bowe of the Massachusetts General Hospital will handle Hitchman's case. I am confident that in another season Hitch will be playing in his 1929 form for the Bruins."

Hitchman played three more seasons for the Bruins. Halfway through 1933–34, Hitchman retired and left the organization to become the coach for the Boston Cubs of the Canadian-American Hockey league. Upon his retirement, the Bruins retired Hitchman's No. 3. It was the first number the organization retired, and only the second in the NHL after the Maple Leafs declared no other player would wear Ace Bailey's No. 6.

34

OWNERSHIP'S CHANGE OF DIRECTION

By 2006, Jeremy Jacobs' most high-profile holding was withering. The Bruins, one of primary pieces of Jacobs' Delaware North conglomerate, had devolved into an also-ran. They were struggling that season, having traded captain Joe Thornton to San Jose on November 30, 2005. The team that was poised to make a deep run in 2003–04, the previous season of on-ice play (the 2004–05 lockout claimed the entire year), had been disassembled after management's miscalculations on the league's landscape following labor unrest. The FleetCenter, which Jacobs had financed with his own money to replace Boston Garden, was not close to selling out. The fans were voicing their displeasure in the best way possible: by staying at home and not watching on NESN, the network Jacobs partially owned.

Jacobs' management style of staying behind the curtain from his headquarters in Buffalo was about to change. He had no other choice.

Jacobs never intended for his investment to run aground. In 1975, as president of Sportsystems, Jacobs bought the Bruins from the Storer Broadcasting Company for $10 million. Jacobs was a hockey fan. But he purchased the Bruins because it was a sound business decision to buy an Original Six franchise and one of the league's most storied arenas. Sportsystems was in the concessions business, and hockey fans could be counted on to spend their money on hot dogs, popcorn, and beer, especially when watching an entertaining product.

"I hope to make the Bruins an artistically sound product, presented in a place where it is enjoyable and pleasant to watch," Jacobs told the *Boston Globe* shortly after taking ownership of the team.

They were just that, even amid the departure of Bobby Orr following the 1975–76 season. Jacobs' paychecks funded the raucous play of Terry O'Reilly, Brad Park, Mike Milbury, the hockey decisions of general manager Harry Sinden, and the coaching (plus sharp wardrobe) of Don Cherry. Fans couldn't get enough of

GOING OUTSIDE

On January 1, 2016, at Foxborough's Gillette Stadium, Jeremy Jacobs became the first NHL owner to host two Winter Classics. Six years earlier, Jacobs, the Bruins, and the Red Sox welcomed the Flyers to Fenway Park.

The Bruins fared better in their first iteration of the outdoor game. After heading into overtime tied at 1–1, Marco Sturm scored the winning goal on Michael Leighton to give the Bruins a 2–1 win. Earlier in the game, Shawn Thornton and Dan Carcillo squared off in the first fight in Winter Classic history. It capped a festive two-day event that featured iconic players Bobby Orr and Bobby Clarke taking to the Fenway Park ice for the ceremonial faceoff in the alumni game.

The Bruins and Canadiens were excited to take their rivalry outside in 2016. But the game turned out to be a dud for the Bruins. Even though Claude Julien dressed in a Bill Belichick–inspired hoodie, the Bruins' coach could not take any luck from his Patriots counterpart. The Canadiens laid a 5–1 pounding on the Bruins, backstopped by local goalie Mike Condon, who grew up in nearby Holliston.

the Lunchpail AC, even if the crew fell short in their chase of the Stanley Cup.

The pursuit continued as the roster turned over and turned into the teams of Ray Bourque, Cam Neely, and a rotating crew of coaches (Cherry, Fred Creighton, Gerry Cheevers, Butch Goring, O'Reilly, Milbury, Rick Bowness, Brian Sutter, Steve Kasper, Pat Burns, Mike Keenan) that Sinden perpetually hired and fired—an approach, in hindsight, the GM regretted. Amid the turnover behind the bench, Jacobs gave his approval by trusting Sinden to do his job.

"I think that was my weakness," Sinden said. "I acted too quickly on some of them. They need time. I was a little too spontaneous. We were in first place when I fired Freddy Creighton. But I liked the coaches. I liked a lot of then. Strangely enough, I liked Steve Kasper. He got a bad rap here. Terry, when he left, had family problems. I told him at time, 'You're on your way.' He had to go out and learn coaching like we all did. He was on his way to becoming a really good coach. I think he would have been. Cheevers was good too. I probably reacted a bit too quick."

By 2006, Sinden had moved on to president, with longtime apprentice Mike O'Connell having assumed stewardship as GM. Their moves weren't working. They hadn't worked for a long time.

The FleetCenter, the Garden's replacement, opened for the 1995–96 season. Opponents found it a far friendlier building than its predecessor. From 1996–2006, it hosted just seven rounds of playoff hockey. It was empty in 1997, 2000, 2001, and 2006 when the Bruins failed to make the playoffs. Of course, it was dark for an entire season without hockey in 2004–05. In this context, Jacobs was not pleased when the 2005–06 version tripped over its skates at the start of the season.

"As ownership, you're to blame, aren't you? The ultimate guy is the buck stops with me," Jacobs told the *Boston Globe* in November of 2005. "Now how I got there, I don't know. I've got to tell you, I had high, high hopes. I thought we did a great job assessing and accumulating these players and it hasn't come to pass that way. We all bear a certain amount of blame but I think I did everything they wanted me to do in so far as giving them the players that they wanted. To some extent, I feel I fulfilled my obligation. But to another extent, maybe I didn't. Maybe I should've played a little different role."

It would be a more active one. On March 25, 2006, O'Connell was fired. Ray Shero, the Bruins' original target as O'Connell's replacement, chose Pittsburgh instead of Boston. On May 26, the Bruins hired Peter Chiarelli, then assistant GM in Ottawa. Sinden became senior adviser to Jacobs, an honorary title. Sinden was no longer involved in hockey operations.

Chiarelli was technically under Ottawa's employ on July 1. Whether it was Chiarelli or interim GM Jeff Gorton, it was Jacobs' checkbook that opened to sign Zdeno Chara and Marc Savard as free agents for a total commitment of $57.5 million. They would be the cornerstones of the Bruins' rebuild. Under Chiarelli's watch, the Bruins became a team that spent to the cap instead of squeezing their players. Chiarelli's team-building philosophy paid off in 2011, when the Bruins won the Stanley Cup, Jacobs' first in 36 years of ownership.

In January of 2015, Jacobs ceded day-to-day control of the Bruins to son Charlie Jacobs, who assumed the title of CEO. Jeremy Jacobs remains the chairman of the NHL's board of governors. On December 17, 2015, Jacobs was awarded the Lester Patrick Award for outstanding service to hockey in the United States.

"This is over the top in my life," Jacobs said of the honor. "This is an experience I never anticipated. It's extraordinarily flattering. It's humbling. Look at the group I'm included with that's so special to me. Guys like Sinden and [Cam] Neely and [Brian] Burke. There's some great guys, great functioning people in the league today, that have had a great role in USA Hockey. I'm very flattered to be a part of it."

35

MR. ZERO

At first, the Bruins did not have immediate plans for Frank Brimsek. General manager Art Ross knew that one day, he would need a replacement in goal for Tiny Thompson. But Thompson's successor would not be needed right away. So in October of 1937, when Ross signed Brimsek out of the Eastern Amateur Hockey League, the former Pittsburgh Yellowjackets goalie did not report to Boston. Brimsek's destination was Providence, where he'd serve his minor league apprenticeship until his services were needed up top.

That came sooner rather than later. By the fall of 1938, Thompson was 35 years old. Thompson's five-game run to win the Stanley Cup took place nine seasons earlier, a long time for a goalie. Both Thompson and the Bruins knew he did not many top-flight years left.

An injury did not help Thompson's cause. On October 30, during an intrasquad scrimmage, a puck glanced above Thompson's right eye. The Bruins did not want to take any chances with Thompson in the season opener against Toronto. Brimsek, who was originally supposed to play in a game for Providence, made his NHL debut on November 3 against the Maple Leafs. The Bruins won 3 –2 with Brimsek in goal instead of Thompson.

Ross had liked what he had seen in Brimsek before. The native of Eveleth, Minnesota, backstopped Providence to the Calder Cup in 1937–38. The Reds goalie was named a First Team All-Star.

GOALTENDING'S EVOLUTION

Frank Brimsek was a standup goalie, under control and in position and square to shots. More than half a century later, Tuukka Rask took to the crease Brimsek once protected and played it in a fashion he would find unrecognizable as well as unplayable.

Many things have progressed in hockey. No position has accelerated more in terms of knowledge, technology, and athleticism than goaltending. The gear that Rask wears is bigger and lighter than the equipment that protected Brimsek from pucks. As a result, Rask moves around the ice faster and with more grace than his predecessor. Rask goes down on his knees to stop pucks and progresses from there, rarely getting back on his skates to reset for the next flurry of attacks. In contrast, Brimsek had to strap on lightweight, ballooning gear. He didn't even wear a mask. He had to rely more on positioning and reflexes to do his job.

But while Ross considered Brimsek the future of Bruins goaltending, he wasn't sure if he was ready to assume the full-time position by 1938–39, his first NHL season. Brimsek's start to his NHL career convinced Ross to make a difficult but necessary transaction. On November 28, 1938, Ross moved Thompson to Detroit for $15,000, primarily because he thought so highly of Brimsek.

"We regret that we were forced to dispose of Tiny," Ross said in *Art Ross: The Hockey Legend Who Built the Bruins*, "but we realize it was to his advantage. He's good for at least five more seasons with Detroit, where I am sure he will be very happy. But if he remained with us, it would be a matter of only two seasons at the most before we would be forced to replace him with the younger Brimsek, a big-league goalie if I ever saw one."

Ross was correct in his projection of the 23-year-old Brimsek, although Bruins fans fretted at first. With Thompson gone, Brimsek settled into the net full-time. On December 1, Brimsek was in net for a 2–0 loss to Montreal. On the same night, Thompson, as the newest Red Wing, was in goal for Detroit's 4–1 win. Brimsek had not started on the right foot. He would correct that in short order.

On December 4, Brimsek was in goal for the Bruins' 5–0 win over Chicago. Two nights later, Brimsek was scheduled to make his Boston Garden debut against Chicago. He delivered a 2–0 shutout in his first game on home ice.

"I felt I was on trial," Brimsek told the *Boston Globe*. "The eyes of the fans bored holes through me. I could feel their cold breaths on the back of my neck."

The back-to-back shutouts would have more company. By the time Brimsek had started seven games, he had posted six shutouts. Thompson was forgotten. Brimsek gained a nickname that would stick: "Mr. Zero."

The end of Brimsek's rookie season was even better than its beginning. The Bruins got the best of the Rangers in a seven-game semifinal. In the final, Brimsek and the Bruins won the Stanley Cup by beating the Maple Series in four of five games. Brimsek took home all kinds of hardware: the Vezina Trophy as the league's best goalie and the Calder Trophy as the top rookie. He was the first goalie in league history to claim both awards in the same year. He was named a First Team All-Star because of his accomplishments: a 33–9–1 record, 10 shutouts, and a 1.56 goals-against average.

"Of all the goals scored on him this season, which isn't very many," Ross told the *Montreal Gazette*, "I have only seen one that possibly could have been stopped."

Brimsek and the Bruins fell short of the Cup the following year. But they roared back into the final in 1940–41 after beating Toronto in the semifinal, four games to three. The Bruins swept the Red

Wings in four straight to snatch the Cup for the second time in three seasons.

Brimsek's brilliance made the Bruins believe they were set up for a dynastic run. But World War II drew Brimsek as well as some of his best teammates away from the NHL. In 1942, the Kraut Line of Woody Dumart, Milt Schmidt, and Bobby Bauer was called to the Royal Canadian Air Force. A year later, Brimsek joined the U.S. Coast Guard, where he played for the U.S. Coast Guard Cutters.

In 1945–46, Brimsek returned to the Bruins. But he was not the same following his service. The Bruins lost to the Canadiens in the final, four games to one. It was the closest Brimsek would come to chasing his third Cup. The Bruins lost in the semifinal in each of the next three seasons, partly because Mr. Zero was not able to duplicate his earlier heroics.

In September of 1949, the Bruins traded Brimsek to the Blackhawks. He played just one season in Chicago. The Blackhawks finished last and didn't qualify for the playoffs, the only time Brimsek failed to play in the postseason in his career. The disappointment was enough for Brimsek to retire.

The Hockey Hall of Fame did not forget about Brimsek's contributions. In 1966, Brimsek gained entry into the hall, becoming the first American-born goalie to do so.

36

BAD TIMES BEFORE GOOD

In 2003–04, the Bruins had a very good team. Their first line of Mike Knuble, Joe Thornton, and Glen Murray was big, powerful, and skilled. Opponents could not do much to slow down the widebodies once they gained control of the puck deep in the offensive zone. The first-liners had good complementary pieces in Sergei Samsonov, Brian Rolston, and an 18-year-old rookie named Patrice Bergeron. On defense, Nick Boynton, Dan McGillis, Hal Gill, and Sean O'Donnell patrolled the blue line. Rookie Andrew Raycroft (29–18–9, 2.05 goals-against average, .926 save percentage) won the Calder Trophy as the league's top rookie. General manager Mike O'Connell bulked up the roster for the playoffs by adding Sergei Gonchar, Michael Nylander, and Jiri Slegr.

They felt like they had unfinished business after a 3–1 series lead over Montreal in the opening round of the playoffs turned into a seven-and-out at the hands of the Canadiens and future Bruins coach Claude Julien.

But O'Connell and president Harry Sinden were reading the future at the same time as serving as stewards of the 2003–04 Bruins. The

executives did not see anything good on the horizon. They were right.

The NHL went dark in 2004–05 because of a season-scrubbing lockout. O'Connell and Sinden had an idea that labor unrest would not go away quickly. So they pitched a plan to owner Jeremy Jacobs. O'Connell and Sinden believed that whenever hockey returned, good players would be available at discount prices. It would be the Bruins' opportunity to improve a roster that was already pretty good.

The Bruins had chances to re-sign Rolston, Knuble, and Nylander. They did not bring back any of the three because they believed better players would be available in 2005–06. They were partly right. Mike Modano and Peter Forsberg were on the market following the lockout. But neither was interested in signing with Boston. Modano reupped with Dallas. Forsberg signed with Philadelphia.

All of a sudden, the Bruins were in full scramble mode. O'Connell had to fill out his roster with junior varsity choices. While O'Connell re-signed Thornton to a three-year, $20 million extension, he also gave Alexei Zhamnov, who was coming off a 43-game season with Chicago and Philadelphia, a three-year, $12.3 million contract. Zhamnov turned out to be a bust. He appeared in 24 games in 2005–06, scoring just one goal and nine assists before suffering a career-ending ankle injury.

Zhamnov was not O'Connell's only regrettable signing. A 37-year-old Brian Leetch was well past his puck-rushing prime when he agreed to a one-year deal. Massachusetts native Tom Fitzgerald, a former captain in Nashville, had also seen his best days in previous seasons before he joined his hometown club as a 37-year-old. Thirty-six-year-old Shawn McEachern, formerly one of the league's elite burners, did not have all cylinders firing when he came back for

ON THIS DATE

JANUARY 9, 2006

The Bruins recall Tim Thomas from Providence. Thomas, however, requires waivers before reporting to Boston, meaning any team can make a claim. Twenty-nine teams decline.

his second stint in Boston. MacEachern played in 28 games before O'Connell assigned him to Providence. He was bought out the following year and never played in the NHL again. Dave Scatchard lasted just 16 games before O'Connell traded him to the Coyotes for David Tanabe. Brad Isbister, acquired from Edmonton for a fourth-round pick on August 1, 2005, scored just six goals and 17 assists in 58 games.

It was no surprise, then, that the 2005–06 Bruins wheezed out of the gate following their misguided team-building forecast. The low point took place on November 30, 2005, when the Bruins traded Thornton to San Jose for Brad Stuart, Marco Sturm, and Wayne Primeau. They never recovered from the blockbuster. O'Connell lost his job before the conclusion of the regular season. The Bruins missed the playoffs. They were in organizational freefall.

But the tailspin prompted some creative thinking. Before he was fired on March 25, 2006, O'Connell re-signed Tim Thomas and P.J. Axelsson, two core players who would become future champions. On March 9, he traded Samsonov to Edmonton for Yan Stastny, Marty Reasoner, and a 2006 second-round selection. Three months later, the Bruins would use the pick to draft Milan Lucic. Such creativity was very much needed for an organization that had gone stale and predictable. They needed new thinking and a fresh approach.

The Bruins considered interim GM Jeff Gorton as O'Connell's full-time replacement. They interviewed former Nashville assistant GM Ray Shero. After Shero went to Pittsburgh instead, the Bruins hired Ottawa assistant GM Peter Chiarelli on May 26, 2006. Gorton would become Chiarelli's assistant GM. Sinden would become senior adviser to Jacobs. Chiarelli would be in charge of hockey operations.

Of all the changes, the biggest was with shifting Sinden to an advisory role. Sinden, who became GM on October 5, 1972, had his hands on every personnel decision for over 30 years. He was in charge of Jacobs' checkbook, and was not quick to open it.

Chiarelli was respectful of Sinden's history, both within the organization and the sport. But Chiarelli had no intentions of running every decision past the Hockey Hall of Fame Player. The new regime would be proactive in signing players, building a welcoming environment for prospective Bruins, and investing in developing prospects.

That June, with Chiarelli still under contract with Ottawa, Gorton pulled off a bank job by acquiring Rask from Toronto for Raycroft. At the draft, under the watch of director of amateur scouting Scott Bradley, the Bruins hit a four-bagger by picking Phil Kessel, Lucic, and Brad Marchand.

The Bruins did not do well during their first season of transition. They finished in 13th place in the East. Chiarelli fired coach Dave Lewis after one season. But they had started a process that resulted in seven straight postseason appearances and one Stanley Cup. Changes needed to take place for success to happen.

37

DESIGNING A CUP

The Bruins were reeling. In 2010, the Flyers had turned them into the third team in NHL history to gag away a seven-game playoff series after snatching a 3–0 lead. Everything was in question, from the roster composition to the coaching to the playing style. Chiarelli, then in his fourth season as Bruins GM, could have steered the whole thing sideways.

He made some changes. On June 22, 2010, Chiarelli sent Dennis Wideman, a 2010 first-round pick, and a 2011 third-rounder to the Panthers for Nathan Horton and Gregory Campbell. Four days later, Chiarelli traded Vladimir Sobotka to St. Louis for prospect David Warsofsky.

But Chiarelli did not blow up the roster that cratered against the Flyers. Instead, he put his faith in his players.

On June 4, the Bruins re-signed Shawn Thornton to a two-year extension. A day later, Dennis Seidenberg agreed to four more years as a Bruin. On June 24, Chiarelli extended Johnny Boychuk for two more seasons. On June 28, Mark Recchi signed a one-year extension. On July 1, the first day of free agency, Daniel Paille signed a two-year extension.

Chiarelli believed in most of his group. He didn't punt them out of town. He was confident he had made the right decisions by bringing them to Boston in the first place.

Chiarelli's approach was consistent with the thinking that brought him to Boston via Ottawa on May 26, 2006. After sacking former GM Mike O'Connell, the Bruins were looking for a young, savvy, and patient problem-solver to execute a prompt turnaround and bolster the organization long-term. They missed out on Ray Shero, who took the Pittsburgh job after interviewing the Bruins. But they landed Chiarelli, then the assistant GM in Ottawa.

Chiarelli had ties to Boston. He attended Harvard for four seasons and was the Crimson captain in 1986–87. He was a Harvard teammate of ex-Bruin Don Sweeney, who he would hire as director of player development. From a distance, Chiarelli watched the team of his college town become irrelevant.

"I want to introduce a new, fresh culture to this organization," Chiarelli told the *Boston Globe*. "I want players to want to play here. I want players to want to stay here. I want players to move their families here. I want them to be proud, I want them to be proud to have the Boston Bruins logo on their chest. In my experience as an agent, I got to know the concerns of players. My experience in management, your main objective is to win. Sometimes you lose sight of these other things the players are thinking. I think because I've experience both I will be able to draw them both together and unite a common, strong bond toward a winning tradition."

One of Chiarelli's first decisions was to inform coach Mike Sullivan he would not be back in 2006–07. Chiarelli replaced Sullivan with Dave Lewis, the longtime Red Wings assistant. Chiarelli believed Lewis' experience under Scotty Bowman made him the right man as Sullivan's replacement.

Chiarelli was wrong. Even though the Bruins had landed help immediately on the free agent market by signing Zdeno Chara and Marc Savard on July 1, 2006, the two additions couldn't help lead their new club to the playoffs. On June 15, 2007, Chiarelli fired Lewis after just one season into a four-year contract. Their shortcomings weren't Lewis' fault. As a first-year GM, Chiarelli committed blunders too. Some of his signings included fringe NHLers such as Petr Tenkrat, Jeff Hoggan, Wade Brookbank, and Nathan Dempsey. He acquired Brandon Bochenski from Chicago for prospect Kris Versteeg. Bochenski didn't do much as a Bruin and gained more career traction in the KHL. Versteeg won two Stanley Cups with Chicago.

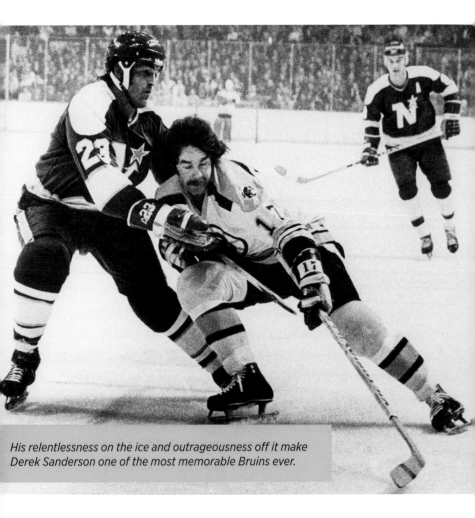

His relentlessness on the ice and outrageousness off it make Derek Sanderson one of the most memorable Bruins ever.

Chiarelli turned what was then his biggest mistake into a move he described as the best one of his Bruins career. On June 21, 2007, six days after Lewis was fired, Claude Julien was introduced as the 27th coach in Bruins history. The Bruins returned to the playoffs in Julien's first season. Julien brought structure and accountability to the Bruins. Chiarelli, meanwhile, gave Julien the players he needed.

Andrew Ference and Chuck Kobasew, ex-Flames Chiarelli had acquired in 2007 for Brad Stuart and Wayne Primeau, became core players for Julien. So did Dennis Wideman, who arrived the year before via St. Louis for Brad Boyes, and Aaron Ward, an ex-Ranger acquired for Paul Mara. Chiarelli signed Thornton, who had won the Cup with Anaheim the year before, as his enforcer. Chiarelli gave the green light to keeping Milan Lucic in Boston as a 19-year-old instead of returning him to junior hockey. The GM was putting the foundational pieces in place.

The Bruins ended Julien's first season with a first-round exit against the Canadiens. They had no such end in 2008–09. The team Chiarelli was building was taking off.

The team that finished atop the Eastern Conference in the regular season breezed through the Canadiens with a four-game sweep in the first round of the playoffs. Mark Recchi, acquired prior to the trade deadline from Tampa Bay with a second-round pick for Matt Lashoff and Martins Karsums, blended neatly into the lineup. Blake Wheeler, a free agent signing after he declined to sign with the Coyotes, his original draft team, was an important third-line wing.

The Bruins lost to Carolina in overtime of Game 7 in the second round. But the team was in good position to make another run. Julien won the Jack Adams Trophy as the league's best coach. Chara won the Norris Trophy as the NHL's best all-around defenseman. Tim

Thomas nabbed the first of two Vezina Trophies as the league's ace goalie.

Then came another second-round exit in 2009–10. It was a far more calamitous ending than the halt to the previous season's march.

So Chiarelli and his colleagues evaluated what they had. They identified what they were missing. Most important, they didn't panic and chuck a grenade into the dressing room.

During training camp of 2010–11, the Bruins retreated to Stowe, Vermont, for teambuilding exercises. Chiarelli wanted his players to decamp from Boston and address their failure against the Flyers. The team grew closer during their season-opening trip to Belfast and Prague as part of the league's Premiere Games initiative in Europe. While overseas, Chiarelli signed Bergeron and Chara, two of his important players, to long-term extensions.

As the season rolled on, Chiarelli believed the group could do good things in the playoffs. They had star stuff in goal in Thomas, who had rebounded following off-season hip surgery. Chara was a shutdown presence. Bergeron and David Krejci were doing heavy lifting in the middle to compensate for Savard, who was unavailable at the start of the season because of post-concussion syndrome and knocked out once more with a head injury, this time for good, on January 22, 2011.

But they were missing a catalyst on the power play. Chiarelli had long kept eyes on Toronto's Tomas Kaberle, the smooth-moving man-up specialist. A trade for Kaberle involving Kessel in June of 2009 was turfed because of a miscommunication between Chiarelli and then-Toronto GM Brian Burke. Chiarelli also wanted to add depth up front.

On February 11, Chiarelli acquired Chris Kelly from the Senators. Chiarelli knew Kelly well from their days together in Ottawa. Kelly

BEST FREE AGENTS

It remains unclear whether it was Peter Chiarelli, still in Ottawa at the time, or interim GM Jeff Gorton who made the decision to chase Zdeno Chara. But with Gorton managing the day-to-day affairs, the Bruins won the Chara sweepstakes on July 1, 2006, when they signed him to a five-year, $37.5 million contract. Landing Chara as an unrestricted free agent helped the Bruins begin their revival.

Other smart signings in the draft era: Mike Milbury (1974), Tim Thomas (2001), Marc Savard (2006), and Blake Wheeler (2008), and Jarome Iginla (2014). The primary teambuilding tools are drafting and developing, while trades are effective ways to improve as well. But deployed smartly, dollars can help bring necessary free agents into the fold.

would become an important third-line center and penalty killer. A week later, Chiarelli was closing in on Kaberle. But he had to clear cap space first to bring Kaberle on board. On February 18, while the Bruins were in Ottawa, Chiarelli traded Wheeler and Mark Stuart to Atlanta for Rich Peverley and Boris Valabik. Wheeler and Stuart were at the team's hotel when Chiarelli delivered the news. They returned to Scotiabank Place to retrieve their gear and join their new team.

Later that day, with Wheeler and Stuart off the books, Chiarelli landed his man. He gave up prospect Joe Colborne, a 2011 first-round pick, and a 2012 second-rounder for Kaberle. The defenseman traveled from Toronto to Ottawa after the trade and played in the Bruins' 4–2 win over the Senators.

"It was an important piece for us to get, and obviously we had to pay a price," Chiarelli said. "Joe is going to be a good player in the NHL. He's progressing nicely and he's a real good kid. We felt the time was right with our team. With the number of assets we've had the last two years, with picks and prospects, it's a testament to the amateur staff and pro staff. We accumulated prospects through pro scouting. We were in a good position to make this transaction. The cupboard is still very well stocked. It's a strong message to our team and to our fans that we want to win and we want to be successful."

Without the acquisitions, it's doubtful the Bruins would have survived four rounds of postseason hockey. The margins of error could not have been thinner against Montreal, Tampa Bay, and Vancouver, who all gave the Bruins seven-game fights. The new Bruins complemented the core group to best the Canucks and deliver the first Cup to Boston since 1972.

It would be Chiarelli's finest work. The Bruins stumbled against the Capitals in the first round of 2012 playoffs. The next year, after rallying against Toronto in the first round, the Bruins marched through the Rangers and Penguins to go head to head against Chicago in the Stanley Cup Final. The Bruins came up two wins short of claiming their second Cup in three seasons.

That summer, Chiarelli made his boldest move by trading Tyler Seguin to Dallas. It would be the worst deal of his career. Short term, Seguin's departure was mitigated by the signing of future Hall of Fame Player Jarome Iginla to a bonus-heavy contract. Iginla quickly found a home next to Lucic and Krejci. With Tuukka Rask rounding into a Vezina-winning goalie, the Bruins finished the regular season with the most points in the league. They dispatched the Red Wings in the first round of the playoffs. But they had no answers for Carey Price and the underdog Canadiens in the second round.

It would be the last time Chiarelli made the playoffs. Iginla had moved on to Colorado for a better deal than the cap-strapped Bruins could offer. Prior to 2014–15, the Bruins' tightness against the salary cap forced Chiarelli to trade Johnny Boychuk on the weekend before the regular-season opener. The Bruins couldn't recover after the move. Krejci played in only 47 games because of groin and knee injuries. Niklas Svedberg failed to be a reliable No. 2 behind Rask, who made a career-high 70 appearances.

Even before the end of the regular season, Chiarelli knew his job was on the line. CEO Charlie Jacobs and president Cam Neely made it clear that everyone was under watch if the Bruins failed to make the playoffs.

"Whether it's Cam or Charlie who said we're all under review, I understand that," Chiarelli said on February 20, 2015. "We've had a lot of success here in my tenure and Claude's tenure. We're having a down year. It's unfortunate that we're under review for one year. But I understand. We've got to make things better."

Things did not improve. The Bruins didn't qualify for the playoffs for the first time since 2007. On April 15, the Bruins fired Chiarelli. Seven straight postseason appearances, one Cup, a second visit to the final, and one Presidents' Trophy were not enough to save Chiarelli's job.

38

TURK

Current Bruins fans are familiar with the job of well-rounded agitator. It is one that Brad Marchand plays well. One of his predecessors, however, was a trailblazer in playing strong, abrasive, under-your-skin hockey. There were few opponents that didn't want to put Derek Sanderson through the glass.

"He wasn't underrated by anybody in hockey," said Harry Sinden. "But he a played a role because of the makeup of those teams where he was out of the offensive limelight more than he should have been. He was a terrific offensive player. He brought a Marchand-on-steroids type of feeling to the team."

On other rosters, Sanderson would have been a go-to forward. His fearlessness put him into net-front situations where it's easier to score from than in perimeter play. Sanderson's hands were good enough to give him 202 career goals in 598 NHL games. But Sanderson fought his way onto a Black-and-Gold roster that had the likes of Phil Esposito, Wayne Cashman, Johnny Bucyk, and Ken Hodge up front. As much as Sanderson's spirit and rambunctiousness might have

qualified him for top-six duty, his more skilled teammates pushed him down the roster.

It was one reason the Bruins won two Stanley Cups in three years. The depth of the team's talent meant Sanderson was often matched against third and fourth lines and bottom-six pairings. It wasn't much competition for the go-go forward. After a two-game throat-clearing with the Bruins in 1966–67, he was returned to junior hockey for the rest of the year. By the following season, Sanderson was better prepared for the rigors of NHL pace. He never played junior again. In 1967–68, after scoring 24 goals and 25 assists, complemented by 98 penalty minutes, Sanderson won the Calder Trophy as the NHL's best rookie. It had not taken Sanderson much time to find his NHL identity.

On the ice, Sanderson was a relentless, nonstop, two-way forward. Off the ice, Sanderson's mouth often operated as quickly as his legs. When Esposito once asked him why he never held back in front of a microphone or a notepad, Sanderson had a prompt response.

"I told him, 'Phil, you score the goals and get the publicity,'" Sanderson wrote in *Crossing the Line: The Outrageous Story of a Hockey Original*. "'Bobby is the greatest player in the game and he gets publicity. I'm a third-line centre. How am I going to get publicity?'"

On his favorite pregame meal: "A steak and a blonde."

On an obscene gesture, for which NHL president Clarence Campbell demanded an explanation: "Oh no, Clarence, you're the one making it obscene. Where I grew up in Niagara Falls, that's the way we say hello to everybody!"

On a Game 2 fight with Ed Giacomin and the Rangers in the 1970 playoffs: "Giacomin told me that William Jennings, the

Rangers' president, put a $5,000 bounty on my head to any Ranger that could maim me." [A total fabrication, by the way.]

The thing about Sanderson was that he backed his mouth with his play. As long as he scored and defended and won faceoffs and killed penalties and stood up for his teammates, his bosses could not criticize him for his yapping. He did plenty of both.

In 1969–70, Sanderson recorded 18 goals, 23 assists, and 118 penalty minutes. In the playoffs, he added nine points and 72 penalty minutes. Without Sanderson, the Bruins might not have won the Cup. He knew it, which gave him greater latitude to push for a better contract and continue his colorful lifestyle. Sanderson held out at the start of 1970–71 before signing a new deal. Off the ice, Sanderson went in on several ventures, including Daisy Buchanan's, a bar that became a Boston landmark. He hosted his own television

FRED CUSICK

Derek Sanderson's most famous partner may have been off the ice. Sanderson served as the color analyst for Fred Cusick, the Bruins' television play-by-play announcer, on Channel 38. Cusick also served as the team's radio announcer. Cusick served the Bruins in both capacities from 1952 through 1997. He remains known as the voice of the Bruins since his death in 2009.

"What I remember most about Fred was his style and passion—his ability to capture the excitement of the game through his voice," said radio play-by-play announcer Dave Goucher. "His voice when a big moment happened or when a big goal was scored. His ability to rise to the occasion when the game called for it. I still get goosebumps when I hear his call of Brad Park's OT goal to beat Buffalo in Game 7 of '83. You knew he was going to be there all winter long. Nobody did it better than him."

show. Sanderson was Johnny Carson's guest on the *Tonight Show*. He even made a brief appearance in an X-rated movie in Canada, although he was not in a starring role.

Sanderson and the Bruins ran headfirst into Ken Dryden and the Canadiens in the 1971 playoffs. But they reloaded to chase another Cup in 1972. Coach Tom Johnson deployed Sanderson in his usual role a fearsome checker. To finish the series, Sanderson went up against Jean Ratelle, Rod Gilbert, and Vic Hadfield. In Game 6, Sanderson helped to keep the Rangers' top line scoreless, while Gerry Cheevers posted a shutout as the Bruins won the Cup for the second time in three seasons.

Then the World Hockey Association came calling. The Philadelphia Blazers offered Sanderson a five-year, $2.65 million blockbuster. The Bruins were offering $80,000. Sanderson had no choice but to accept the Blazers' offer. Sanderson's departure coincided with those of Gerry Cheevers, John McKenzie, Ted Green, and Ed Westfall. The team that was in the dynasty conversation was to be no more.

Sanderson's time in Philadelphia lasted just eight games, to say nothing of five years. The floundering Blazers promptly bought out Sanderson's contract. Sanderson returned to the Bruins, scoring 15 points in 25 games, but the team lost to the Rangers in the 1973 playoffs. The heydays of Sanderson and the Big Bad Bruins were over.

By March of 1974, Sanderson was done for good. After fighting with teammate Terry O'Reilly, Sanderson was suspended for the rest of the season and for the playoffs. The Bruins could have used Sanderson in the postseason, when they fell to the Flyers in the final in six games. But Sanderson had burned any good will he had left. After years of bad behavior, including alcohol and drug abuse, the organization had had enough.

Sanderson lost control of his life. By the time he was 31, Sanderson found himself living temporarily in Central Park, trying to convince a fellow down-on-his-luck inhabitant to share a drink. Friends, including Orr, his former teammate, helped Sanderson. In retrospect, Sanderson was fortunate to leave the game with only bad hips. There were times he could have died. Compared to death, an early exit from hockey and a lifetime of limping were a better alternative.

39

OIL SPILLS

In 1988, the Oilers broke Ray Bourque's heart. The franchise defenseman had advanced to the Stanley Cup Final for the first time in his career, only to have the Edmonton powerhouse blow through the Bruins in four straight games.

But in another way, Bourque and the Bruins had done something great that year. In the second round of the playoffs, the Bruins had punted the Canadiens out of the postseason. It was the first time in 45 years the Bruins had beaten the Canadiens in the playoffs.

"Every summer, all summer long, I'd hear, 'What happened? You guys lost again,'" said Bourque, a Montreal native, upon returning to his hometown. "That year, nobody said anything. It was the quietest summer I ever had."

Bourque and the Bruins might have deserved better that year and two seasons later. They were very good in both years. They just had the unfortunate fate of running into one of the NHL's dynasties each time. Not many clubs could have contended with Wayne Gretzky, Mark Messier, Jari Kurri, Steve Smith, Jeff Beukeboom, and Grant Fuhr in

1988. By 1990, Gretzky had been traded to Los Angeles, but even the departure of the game's greatest player ever did not diminish the behemoth that ran over the Bruins for the second time in three seasons.

But upon reflection, the Bruins finally were able to stick their chests out a little further in 1988 after 45 years of tail-tucking against their biggest rivals. For 18 straight series, including four in a row from 1984 to '87, it had always been something: Ken Dryden, too many men, or a simply overwhelming roster that gave bleu, blanc, et rouge the yearly advantage over Black and Gold.

That ended in 1988.

"After that," Bourque said, "we started to have some success."

Under coach Terry O'Reilly, the Bruins went 44–30–6 during the regular season. A 27-year-old Bourque (17 goals, 64 assists) was riding in the sweet spot of his career, with enough experience on his resume and still plenty of juice in his tree-trunk legs. Cam Neely (42 goals) broke the 40-goal threshold for the first of four times. Glen Wesley, the No. 3 pick from 1987, jumped from junior to the NHL to play 79 dependable games as a 19-year-old. The oft-injured Gord Kluzak, the first overall pick in 1982, was healthy enough to play 66 games and score 37 points. Near the end of the season, the Bruins picked up reinforcements in Craig Janney and Andy Moog.

After a six-game battle against Buffalo in the first round of the playoffs, the Canadiens were up next. Montreal had a terrific blend of talent: skill in Bobby Smith, Mats Naslund, and Stephane Richer; snarl on the back end in Larry Robinson and Chris Chelios; wit up front in Guy Carbonneau and Bob Gainey; and the unflappable Patrick Roy in net.

The Canadiens started the here-we-go-again moaning when they won Game 1. But Reggie Lemelin, who replaced Moog for Game 2, helped to stabilize his team in a 4–3 Game 2 win. Three wins later,

WORKING IN TANDEM

Within a seven-month span in 1987 and 1988, the Bruins made two important acquisitions that would help both of their Stanley Cup runs. Both of the upgrades were in goal.

On August 13, 1987, the Bruins signed Reggie Lemelin as a free agent. The 32-year-old goalie made a name for himself in Calgary. But the Flames were ready to hand over the crease to Mike Vernon, five years younger than Lemelin.

In 1987–88, his first season in Boston, Lemelin helped backstop the Bruins to a second-place finish in the division. By the end, Lemelin got some help. On March 8, 1988, the Bruins acquired Andy Moog from Edmonton for Geoff Courtnall, Bill Ranford, and a second-round pick. With Moog and Lemelin in goal, the Bruins beat the Canadiens in the playoffs before losing to Edmonton.

Two years later, when most teams were going with an ace, Lemelin and Moog served as an equal tandem. Again, they fell short to the Oilers in the final. But they would have never advanced to the Cup without either of their steady goalies.

the Bruins were almost in disbelief at what had happened: they had finally beaten the Canadiens.

"That's history," Keith Crowder told the *Boston Globe* of the 45-year streak. "That's [expletive] history. Now they can't say any of that stuff about us they say every year. It's all gone. There are no more flukes. There are no more jinxes. Nothing."

After a seven-game tilt against New Jersey in the conference final, the Bruins went toe-to-toe with the Oilers. It did not take long for Edmonton to establish its dominance. Three games later, the Bruins were facing elimination at Boston Garden. Midway through the second period with the score tied at 3–3, the lights went out at the creaky Garden, forcing the league to scrap the game and reschedule it to be played in Edmonton. It only put off the inevitable: a 6–3 Edmonton win and a four-and-out for the Bruins.

The Bruins only won one round the following season before the Canadiens got their revenge. But the Bruins reloaded for 1989–90, going 46–25–9. Under first-year coach Mike Milbury, the Bruins were even better than they were two years earlier. Neely, who scored 55 goals, played like a menace, with Janney threading him pucks. Bourque was at the height of his powers. Lemelin and Moog formed one of the league's most consistent puck-stopping tandems.

But the Bruins nearly exited without winning a single round following a dangerous encounter with the underdog Whalers.

"We got a freaking tiger by the tail," Milbury said. "We were their Goliath."

It did not help the Bruins that Bourque went missing for Games 2 through 6 because of a hip injury. For Milbury, Bourque was his ace. He started every game. If it was a close game, Bourque was on the ice for every last minute. Now the Bruins were entering a do-or-die Game 7 without their captain—or so they thought.

"He came to the rink on the day of the game at around 4:30 and took a little twirl around the ice," Milbury said. "He came to see me and said, 'I think I can play.' I said, 'Well OK, let me think about that.'"

Of course, there was nothing for Milbury to think about. Bourque was in. The Bruins won Game 7 3–1. The Bruins, energized by Bourque's return and the first-round battle against their New England neighbors, dispatched the Canadiens in five games. They needed one less to end Washington's season. It set them up for a rematch against the Oilers.

The Bruins wanted to set the tone in Game 1. They did in all the wrong ways, losing in triple overtime 3–2. Wesley missed a wide-open net in double overtime when Bill Ranford was down and out in the Edmonton crease. In third OT, Petr Klima, a benchwarmer for most of the night, ended the game at 1:23 AM the following morning. The gut-punch allowed the Oilers to claim Game 2 in a rout 7–2.

"It was sad to end it the way it ended," Milbury said. "The triple overtime game, Wesley with an open net on his backhand—he could have turned and gone to his forehand, he was so wide open and had so much time. He just missed it. Then [expletive] Petr Klima, on the bench for three-and-a-half hours, scores the goal. That was a measure of their depth. Their fourth line was [Adam] Graves, [Martin] Gelinas, and Joe Murphy. That's the fourth line. We gave it a good run. If we'd won the first game, maybe we would have extended it. But they had more talent."

40

A GAME-CHANGING HIT

On March 7, 2010, the Bruins were visiting the Penguins. They were down in the third period 2–1. Marc Savard tried to change that.

Throughout his career, Savard was a pass-first playmaker. Upon arriving in Boston in 2006 as an unrestricted free agent via Atlanta, Savard settled into his dishing role, much like predecessors Joe Thornton and Adam Oates.

But on this day and in this situation, after taking a pass from linemate Milan Lucic, Savard tried to tie the game by winging a shot on goal. Savard missed. Matt Cooke did not.

As Savard snapped off a wrist shot on Pittsburgh goalie Marc-Andre Fleury, Cooke approached from the right side. Once Savard let the puck fly, Cooke struck. The Pittsburgh winger drove his left shoulder into the right side of Savard's head. Savard helicoptered in the air and dropped to the ice unconscious.

Savard had suffered a major concussion. Referees Marc Joannette and Tim Peel did not consider Cooke's hit worthy of a penalty. Cooke was not subject to supplemental discipline from

the league. According to the rule book, Cooke did not do anything wrong.

Cooke's history, however, said otherwise. By then, he had established a reputation for borderline play. He was suspended for two games in 2004 for spearing Minnesota's Matt Johnson. In 2009, the NHL tagged Cooke with a two-game suspension for injuring Carolina's Scott Walker. The following season, Cooke was banished for two games for elbowing the Rangers' Artem Anisimov. By the time he clobbered Savard, Cooke was well known around the league for being a vicious, hit-to-hurt player. None of his previous blows, however, staggered an opponent so severely like Savard.

The Bruins center was immobilized on the ice by medical staff. He was wheeled off on a stretcher and transported to a Pittsburgh hospital. While the Bruins left Pittsburgh after the game, Savard remained in the hospital overnight. He flew to Boston the following day despite feeling the signature symptoms of post-concussion syndrome: fatigue, headaches, sensitivity to light.

It was not Savard's first concussion. He had been the victim of head shots during his junior and professional careers. But it was the worst one he had suffered. Because of his symptoms, Savard didn't play another regular season game in 2010. Surprisingly, he felt well enough to return for the second round of the playoffs against the Flyers.

While Savard's life changed because of the hit, so did the league's acceptance of head shots, albeit not immediately. Following the incident, then–general manager Peter Chiarelli participated in the GM meetings in Boca Raton, Florida, where he lobbied NHL disciplinarian Colin Campbell to discipline Cooke for the hit.

But on March 10, 2010, Campbell declared that Cooke would not be suspended. There was nothing in the rule book that Campbell could use to discipline Cooke. Earlier that season, Philadelphia's

ON THIS DATE

AUGUST 1, 2011

Marc Savard spends the day with the Stanley Cup in Peterborough, Ontario, where the Ottawa native makes his home. Savard's name is engraved on the Cup after the Bruins file a petition with the league.

Mike Richards walloped Florida's David Booth with an open-ice hit. Booth missed 45 games because of a concussion. Richards was not suspended.

"What I tried to convince the hockey ops staff was to take it outside of the current rule," Chiarelli said. "Use the repeat offender criteria and implement an infraction on an intent to injure. That infraction and the repeat offender should distinguish it from the Richards hit. They didn't want to."

But the incident served as the centerpiece for discussion among the 30 GMs. They concluded that such hits had to be subject to discipline. Following the meetings, the GMs gave the green light to a proposal that would be presented to the NHL's competition committee later in 2010. Upon its approval, it would become known as Rule 48: "A lateral, back-pressure, or blindside hit to an opponent where the head is targeted and/or the principal point of contact is not permitted. A violation of the above will result in a minor or major penalty and shall be reviewed for possible supplemental discipline."

Culture change was inevitable. The league was starting to acknowledge the danger of concussions, both immediate and long-term when it came to player safety and health. Lawsuits against the NHL from stricken players would come in future years. The NHL had to act. Savard's injury served as a springboard for change.

"The controversial decision that Colin Campbell made to not suspend Matt Cooke for hitting Marc Savard was a brave one in my mind," former NHL disciplinarian Brendan Shanahan told the *Boston Globe*, "because it didn't break a current rule in the NHL rule book. And by taking the storm that followed, by not just making something up, he actually made a bigger impact on the game of hockey. Two weeks later, there was a brand new rule for an illegal check to the head. He couldn't undo what happened to Marc Savard."

On June 1, 2011, Shanahan replaced Campbell as the league's disciplinarian. Shanahan served as the leader of the NHL's Department of Player Safety, which was launched to start the 2011–12 season. The department was responsible for identifying plays and players subject to supplemental discipline, with an emphasis on coming down swiftly on hits to the head.

Since its creation, the department ruled on several significant incidents. In 2012, Coyotes tough guy Raffi Torres was suspended for 25 games after delivering a head shot to Chicago's Marian Hossa in Game 3 of the Western Conference Quarterfinals. In 2013, the department suspended Buffalo's Patrick Kaleta for 10 games for hitting Columbus' Jack Johnson in the head. In 2015, Torres, who had moved on to San Jose, was suspended for 41 games for hitting Anaheim's Jakob Silfverberg in the head during a preseason game.

The department changed the way players play. It came too late, however, for Savard.

The center scored a goal and two assists in his seven playoff games against Philadelphia in 2010. Both Savard and the organization believed he had recovered from Cooke's hit.

But that summer, Savard was not right. He suffered from symptoms such as headaches, dizziness, and nausea. He was also diagnosed with depression.

"I am definitely going to take my time and make sure that I am 100 percent in every aspect before I even think about playing," Savard told the *Boston Globe* during training camp, in which he did not participate.

By the fall of 2010, Savard was feeling better enough to resume off-ice activities. On December 2, 2010, Savard appeared in his first game of the season, playing 15:45 in an 8–1 rout of Tampa Bay. The center was back, feeling good, and optimistic about his future.

It all ended on January 22, 2011, at Denver's Pepsi Center. Former teammate Matt Hunwick belted Savard into the boards. Ironically, the Bruins had traded Hunwick earlier that season to Colorado to open up a roster spot for Savard.

Savard suffered another concussion on the play. It was the last time he would appear in an NHL game. On February 7, 2011, the Bruins declared Savard's season to be over.

"I think I'm frustrated mostly," said Savard, who appeared pale and tired while discussing his situation. "It's tough to understand why this happens. Obviously the most frustrating thing is to not be able to just know exactly what's going on and how to cure it. I think it's just time and patience. Those are things I feel like I don't have much of. So that makes it tough."

Savard was not present for his team's championship run. The Bruins successfully lobbied the league to have Savard's name etched onto the Cup, even though he did not appear in the playoffs. Once his symptoms failed to wane that summer, his career was over, even though his contract ran through 2017.

"Based on what I see, what I hear, what I read, and what I'm told, it's very unlikely Marc will play again," Chiarelli said. "Now, knowing the uncertainty of this injury, there's always a chance. But based on what I'm told, it's very unlikely he'll play. As an employer, I support him and hope he gets back to living a healthy life."

Savard finished his career with 207 goals and 499 assists in 807 games for the Bruins, Thrashers, Flames, and Rangers. On July 1, 2015, the Bruins traded Savard and Reilly Smith to the Panthers for Jimmy Hayes.

41

LOCAL KID DOES GOOD

At Walpole High School, Mike Milbury was excellent at football, hockey, and baseball. He was good enough to score a scholarship to play hockey at Colgate. Regardless of his skill, Milbury never considered himself worthy of stepping onto the professional ice he considered the ultimate sheet of ice: at Boston Garden alongside the heroes of his childhood.

"I never allowed myself to dream about the Bruins very much," said Milbury. "I played all sports. I was a pretty good baseball player. I dreamed that dream, but I never thought it was within my grasp. As much as we had a pretty good team at Walpole High School, I was going to Colgate. I was thinking, *Maybe I'll go to Europe.* There were a lot of guys going there to make enough money to eat and party for a couple months."

But by July of 1974, Milbury had built up enough of a resume at Walpole High, Colgate, and during a tryout for the Boston Braves to earn an invitation to his hometown team's training camp. Even then, it seemed more like a dream.

"I never allowed myself the fantasy," Milbury said, "that I would play for that team."

His fantasy turned into a 754-game reality, with every NHL appearance taking place in the Black-and-Gold jersey he always admired. Milbury then became the ninth Bruins player to step behind the team's bench. Milbury played and coached with the ferocity and doggedness that dropped him onto the organization's radar in the first place. Few Bruins matched the spirit with which Milbury approached either profession.

"I like to think I was among the people that sustained the image of the team—that being you tried hard every night and did whatever it took," Milbury said. "For those who say you can play without fear, there's fear there. Even the toughest players have fear. You have to find a way to play through it."

Milbury was often the one making his opponents scared. His most productive season was in 1977–78, when he scored eight goals and 30 assists for 38 points in 80 games. He also compiled 151 penalty minutes, a total he would surpass in five other seasons. The rugged defenseman had no reservations about shedding his mitts when necessary, which was quite often when Don Cherry was calling out orders as the Bruins' coach.

Milbury's willingness to fight, however, was a manifestation of the do-anything approach with which he entered the league and stayed in it. His break came in 1974 when he scored a five-game tryout with the Boston Braves, who had seen him participate in the Syracuse Invitational Tournament. After completing his senior season at Colgate, Milbury borrowed a friend's car and drove back home in hopes of making a good professional impression. He played hard. He fought. That summer, the call came. The 22-year-old who was hauling furniture for a summer job had the opportunity to compete for an NHL paycheck.

For his first day of camp, Milbury was placed in the second group. The first group included his idols: Bobby Orr and Phil Esposito. Only that after a long night of lubrication, some of Milbury's stars weren't sprinting to hit the ice.

"The only guy left in the room is Espo," said Milbury, who had arrived hours early for his session. "He's running late. Everybody

DREAMS COME TRUE FOR LOCALS

Ted Donato and Steve Heinze were Black-and-Gold teammates for parts of eight seasons. Donato, a West Roxbury native, scored 119 goals in 528 games as a Bruin. Heinze, who was born in Lawrence and raised in North Andover, scored 131 goals in 515 games. Donato (Harvard) and Heinze (Boston College) were two of the Massachusetts youngsters who achieved their dreams of playing for their hometown team.

Other players raised in Massachusetts who pulled on Black and Gold include Bobby Allen, Shawn Bates, Andy Brickley, Jim Carey, Bobby Carpenter, Jim Craig, Tom Fitzgerald, Hal Gill, Bill Guerin, Jimmy Hayes, Dan LaCouture, Jeff Lazaro, Steve Leach, Paul Mara, Shawn McEachern, Marty McInnis, Mike Milbury, Bob Miller, Jay Miller, Chris Nilan, Billy O'Dwyer, Dave Silk, Frank Simonetti, Kevin Stevens, Bob Sweeney, and Mike Sullivan.

else is on the ice and Phil was fidgeting with his skates. Bobby walked back into the room and said, 'Phil, what the [expletive] are you doing? It's time to get on the ice and practice. It's two minutes to eight, we've got a new coach, we didn't win [expletive] last year, get the [expletive] on the ice.' I'm hiding in the bathroom stall. Here are two of my idols. You knew at the time who was running the show. It was eye-popping, not only for its intensity. The point was made and the point got through to me. It was time to go to work."

Milbury did not make the varsity that year. He was assigned to Rochester of the AHL. Milbury learned the craft of making the front of his net a hostile area, with his stick as well as his fists.

"It was part of the deal back then," Milbury said of fighting. "It became part of my game. I wasn't Terry O'Reilly tough, but I had my fair share. It was a time, too, when being a little bit squirrelly was good playing on defense. They allowed you to express yourself in front of the net more often. I guess I expressed myself pretty well."

Milbury's most colorful expression took place off the ice. On December 23, 1979, at the conclusion of the Bruins' 4–3 win over the Rangers at Madison Square Garden, a fan hit Stan Jonathan and grabbed his stick. Milbury had retreated to the dressing room. But when he learned that O'Reilly had climbed into the stands to address the situation, Milbury felt he had no choice but to follow. Moments later, Milbury entered NHL infamy by clubbing a fan with his own shoe. The NHL suspended O'Reilly for eight games and sat Milbury down for six.

To Milbury, it was a case of sticking up for teammates. Such was the expectation once he pulled the Bruins jersey over his head. It was why Cherry, the bold Canadian, took a liking to the American, one of the few U.S. players in the league at the time. The two regularly commuted to and from practice.

"I think he saw a bit of a longshot and an underdog," Milbury said of why he caught Cherry's attention. "I was willing and was a hard worker. I think he saw some of those things in himself. Here's a guy who spent many years in the minor leagues and played all of one National Hockey League game."

Milbury could not help but play hard for Cherry. Milbury expected the same thing after he retired as a player and became a coach. Milbury's initial desire was to enter hockey operations with the Maine Mariners, the Bruins' farm club. But general manager Harry Sinden believed Milbury would be best served coaching as well. Sinden explained that a manager's most important decision was hiring the right coach. Having experience behind the bench, Sinden believed, would serve Milbury well when it came time to hire his own man.

After a two-year AHL apprenticeship, Milbury became the Bruins' coach on May 16, 1989. It did not take Milbury long to make his mark. In Milbury's first season, the Bruins dispatched Hartford, Montreal, and Washington in the playoffs to set up a revenge match against Edmonton in the Stanley Cup Final. The Bruins were tight and talented. Ray Bourque and Cam Neely were at the peak of their powers. Andy Moog and Reggie Lemelin were dependable in goal. But they did not have enough firepower to hang with the mighty Oilers.

"We had fun like Grapes' teams had fun," Milbury said. "Guys went out together. It was a really good group, a fun group to be around, a really hard-working group. It was a magical run."

42

A FIGHT GONE WRONG

There was nothing subtle about the way Ted Green played hockey. At 5'10" and 200 pounds, the defenseman from Eriksdale, Manitoba, was not the biggest player of his era. Nor was he the most skilled. Green's spirit, however, made up for his shortcomings.

Green, originally property of the Canadiens, was claimed by the Bruins in the 1960 intraleague draft. General manager Lynn Patrick identified that the scrappy Green could imbue the Bruins with his bruising element. Patrick was right. Green was a good addition for the Bruins. By the end of the decade, Green had developed into a feared but important player for a team desperate to shake years of losing. Green earned his nickname of "Terrible Ted" the hard way.

"I didn't like the name or the reputation," Green said in *Boston Bruins: Greatest Moments and Players*. "I played hockey hard, and sure I hit, because it was my job to do it. In my younger days, maybe I went out of my way to find a fight, but not later."

Green's fearless play not only took away his chance at lifting the Stanley Cup in 1970. It almost cost him his life.

On September 21, 1969, the Bruins were playing St. Louis in an exhibition game in Ottawa. Green clashed with St. Louis' Wayne Maki. Green and the Blues forward exchanged the usual actions of hockey conflict: punches, slashes, and spears.

A FAMOUS CHALLENGE

The most significant fight in Bruins history never happened. Yes, there was a prelude on December 1, 1977. During a Bruins–North Stars game at Boston Garden, while Terry O'Reilly was laying the lumber to Steve Jensen, John Wensink was doing the same to Alex Pirus.

Wensink, signed as a free agent the year before, was in his first full NHL season. The forward was a good all-around player. In 80 games, Wensink scored 16 goals and 20 assists. But he was a terror when his gloves were off, as Pirus found out that night. Wensink recorded 181 penalty minutes. Most of them were of the five-minute variety.

After getting the best of Pirus, Wensink heard the chatter from the Minnesota bench. Wensink approached the bench, slammed on the brakes, and put out his hands to accept any and all challengers. None took up Wensink on his offer. After several moments of waiting, Wensink turned his back on the North Stars and skated off the ice, but not before he gave several waves of disgust to his opponents.

At the time, stickwork took place occasionally. Players did not wear helmets, so they took care to aim their sticks at less vulnerable body parts. Maki, however, did not take such caution. After taking a slash from Green, Maki clubbed his opponent on the head with his stick.

"As Greenie turned, Maki hit him right smack over the head," teammate Derek Sanderson recalled in Boston Bruins: Greatest Moments and Players. "Teddy went down on his side. He just stretched out on the ice, stunned, although he wasn't bleeding very much."

Maki had done near-lethal damage to Green's head. Upon admittance to Ottawa General Hospital, doctors concluded Green had suffered a fractured skull. The impact of the stick swing had broken several bone fragments and driven them into Green's brain. Green was unable to speak. Even after initial surgery, Green was in trouble. He suffered a hemorrhage, which left him partially paralyzed on his left side.

Green would not play again that season, missing out on the opportunity to hoist the Cup. He would recover from his injuries to resume his career the following season. He did not blame Maki for his injury as much as for the leaguewide acceptance for such hostility. But even before he was completely out of danger, Green acknowledged both he and his counterparts had to change the way they considered violence.

"I hope the [NHL] governors will now, finally, take some strong action against stick swinging," Green told the *Toronto Telegram* while he was still in Ottawa General. "I don't want this thing to happen to anyone else. They must not wait until there is a fatality. Maybe I deserved what I got. Maybe I didn't but the game itself is as much to blame as Ted Green and Wayne Maki. For years hockey has allowed stick fights to continue without doing too much to stamp them out. Some people have even exploited stick fights to sell tickets, to fill their rinks. I've used a stick before not really knowing what it could do. The penalty wasn't enough to make you even think, let alone think twice. It's a violent game and you hit and get hit. Tempers boil and it's a case of him or you."

Doctors inserted a plate in Green's head. They didn't rule out a return to playing. But before then, Green had to answer for his actions. Both Green and Maki were charged with assault causing bodily harm. It was the first criminal case ever filed against NHL players for on-ice actions. Maki had already served a 30-day suspension from the league.

On March 5, 1970, Maki was acquitted, citing self-defense. Green's charge was reduced to common assault. But Green still had to testify in Ottawa Municipal Court. On September 3, 1970, Green was acquitted of his charge. Judge Michael Fitzpatrick ruled that hockey cannot be played without actions that are normally considered assaults off the ice. Green was free to continue his playing career.

Green returned to the NHL with a helmet. He also returned a changed player. The hard-charging, stick-swinging, Terrible Ted had no intentions of taking or inflicting damage like he did that night in Ottawa. He focused on playing strong, physical, and dependable defense. A year away from hockey did not disrupt Green's play. In 1970–71, Green scored five goals and 37 assists in 78 games. A year later, Green recorded a goal and 16 assists in 54 games. At the end, Green claimed the Cup he was unable to chase two years earlier.

The World Hockey Association took notice of Green's comeback. After he won the Cup in 1972, Green left the Bruins and the NHL for the New England Whalers of the WHA. Green never returned to the NHL as a player. After being traded to the Jets of the WHA, Green concluded his playing career in 1979. He then joined Glen Sather in Edmonton, where he served as an assistant coach to his former Bruins teammate. Green and the Oilers won five Cups. Green followed Sather to the Rangers, with whom he concluded his coaching career in 2004. Green didn't suffer any long-term damage because of the injury. Considering how much danger he was in at first, Green was lucky.

43

TRADING THE FUTURE

Phil Kessel had his warts. He was not committed to defense. When he wasn't scoring, he wasn't contributing much else.

But the fifth overall pick in 2006 led the Bruins with 36 goals in 2008–09. Few of his league rivals were blessed with his speed and shot. As such, the Bruins made several attempts to re-sign the right wing upon the expiration of his entry-level contract. None of the offers was good enough for the 21-year-old to put pen to paper.

At the same time, the Maple Leafs wanted Kessel badly. GM Brian Burke was preparing to sign Kessel to an offer sheet. So on September 18, 2009, the Bruins traded Kessel to Toronto for first-round picks in 2010 and 2011, plus a second-rounder in 2010. After landing in Toronto, Kessel agreed to a five-year, $27 million contract.

"Let me be perfectly clear," said GM Peter Chiarelli. "This trade is really about two things. One, it's about a player who did not want to play in Boston. Two, it's about the threat or the perceived threat of an offer sheet."

Kessel was a good young player for the Bruins. During his rookie season, Kessel beat testicular cancer and claimed the league's Bill Masterton Memorial Trophy, awarded annually to the player who best exemplifies perseverance, sportsmanship, and dedication to hockey.

As a second-year NHLer, Kessel played in all 82 games. He dressed for Game 1 of the opening round of the playoffs against the Canadiens, but was a healthy scratch for the next three tilts. He returned for Game 5 and scored. He added two more goals in Game 6.

But by the end of his third season in Boston, Kessel wanted out. The Bruins gave him his wish.

The bounty reflected Toronto's opinion of Kessel. But the Leafs never believed they'd be a lottery team after acquiring Kessel. Throughout 2009–10, Kessel's first season in Toronto, Chiarelli kept one eye on his own team and the other on the Leafs. The privilege of picking Taylor Hall or Tyler Seguin, the presumed top two players in the 2010 NHL Draft, looked like it would become reality.

The Oilers won the lottery and picked Hall. The Bruins' consolation prize was Seguin, a raw but wickedly talented center who had similar gifts to Kessel: high-end speed, creativity, and a deadly shot. In the second round, the Bruins drafted Jared Knight, a solidly built forward projected to become a second- or third-line NHL right wing.

"It feels amazing," Seguin said of being drafted. "I can't really describe it. Maybe it's like winning the Stanley Cup. It's one of the best feelings I've had so far."

Seguin would not have to wait long to learn the feeling of hoisting the Cup. He made the Bruins' roster out of camp that fall. The 18-year-old scored his first NHL goal in his second game. Seguin was a healthy scratch for the first two rounds of the playoffs against Montreal and Philadelphia. He made his playoff debut in Game 1 of the Eastern Conference Final against Tampa Bay and scored a goal

Power forward Milan Lucic was a vital part of the core group of players who carried the Bruins through the 2011 playoffs and to their first Stanley Cup in nearly 40 years.

and an assist. One game later, Seguin lit up the Lightning with two goals and two assists to help the Bruins tie the series 1–1.

By the end of the playoffs, Seguin was riding on the third line with Chris Kelly and Michael Ryder. The 19-year-old had won the Cup. Both Seguin and the Bruins thought there might be others to follow. Nobody questioned his talent. He was learning the game under veterans such as Mark Recchi, Patrice Bergeron, and Zdeno Chara.

Seguin showed so much potential that even before the start of his third season, the Bruins saw fit to give him an extension. Just before the 2012–13 lockout put a halt to leaguewide business, the Bruins signed Seguin to a six-year, $34.5 million deal.

"I see a player who's committed to getting better," Chiarelli said. "I see a player who's already baselining at such a high level. Tyler has things to learn, and he knows that. He knows the things he has to learn and the things he has to be better at. But I see such a high baseline that I think it's the prudent thing to do under the current set of rules. Sometimes we have to make decisions like that, and we made this one with Tyler."

The premature extension may have contributed to the stall in Seguin's development. In 2012–13, upon his return from Biel in Switzerland's National League A, Seguin scored 16 goals and 16 assists. In the playoffs, Seguin scored just one goal and seven assists.

On the ice, the Bruins questioned Seguin's courage and two-way commitment. Off the ice, they were worried about Seguin's lifestyle. While the Bruins were advancing through the playoffs in 2013, Chiarelli and his colleagues in hockey operations were exploring trade possibilities. The chatter expanded during the 2013 NHL Draft. At the time, nothing happened.

"He's got to commit his mind and focus on the one task at hand," Chiarelli said following the first round. "He's got to become more of a professional. And you know what? I can say that about a lot of 21-year-olds. I know he got criticized for playing on the periphery and all that stuff. He did. He's got to commit to being a professional and focusing on the game. He does that, we don't expect him to be crashing and banging. Just play your game."

Nothing at the draft made the Bruins act. Less than a week later, the Bruins got the package they wanted.

On July 4, 2013, the Bruins traded Seguin, Rich Peverley, and Ryan Button to Dallas. The Stars sent back Loui Eriksson, Reilly Smith, Matt Fraser, and Joe Morrow. The Bruins received a responsible three-zone wing in Eriksson. But they lost Fraser to Edmonton on waivers in 2014. After the 2014–15 season, they traded Smith to Florida.

On the other end, the Stars landed a game-breaking center. In his first season in Dallas, Seguin scored 37 goals and 47 assists for 84 points. He immediately found a home on the Stars' top line alongside captain Jamie Benn. They became one of the league's most dangerous offensive tandems.

"You watch players, there were only so many guys who could do what he could do," said Stars GM Jim Nill, who scouted Seguin heavily in junior hockey. "He's got great speed. He's got real quick hands. There's only so many of these guys in this game. He's got that ability. He's still a young guy. There's more growth yet. He's 21 years old. He's still got lots of growth ahead of him. I'm excited about the total package of what he can do."

The Bruins lost the trade. They did not expect Seguin to explode into one of the best centers in the game. Their solace, however, was one of the other components of the Kessel trade. They no longer

WORST TRADES

Through three seasons with Dallas after being traded by the Bruins, Tyler Seguin had scored 107 goals and 234 points in 223 games. The three-year segment has not even seen Seguin reach the peak of his ability. At his pace, Seguin could become a Hall of Fame Player. It was a trade the Bruins will not recover from for a long time, if at all.

Other duds: Tom Fergus to Toronto for Bill Derlago; Ray Bourque and Dave Andreychuk to Colorado for Brian Rolston, Samuel Pahlsson, Martin Grenier, and a first-round pick; Pahlsson to Anaheim for Patrick Traverse and Andrei Nazarov; Joe Thornton to San Jose for Brad Stuart, Marco Sturm, and Wayne Primeau; Kris Versteeg to Chicago for Brandon Bochenski; and Reilly Smith to Florida for Jimmy Hayes and Marc Savard.

had Seguin, the 2010 first-round pick, but they had big plans for Dougie Hamilton, the 2011 first-rounder.

In 2010–11, the Leafs did not get much better. The Bruins didn't mind. They were awaiting the second of two first-round picks owed to them for Kessel. Following the lottery, the Bruins ended up with the ninth pick in 2011. They jumped at drafting Hamilton, a can't-miss blue-line prospect.

At 18 years of age, Hamilton was already 6'5" and pushing 200 pounds. During his draft year, Hamilton scored 12 goals and 46 assists in 67 games for the Niagara IceDogs of the OHL. He was the second defenseman to go in 2011, following Adam Larsson (No. 4 overall to New Jersey). The Bruins were elated.

In Hamilton, the Bruins believed they had drafted Zdeno Chara's replacement as the team's No. 1 defenseman. Hamilton projected to have every tool once he hit his sweet spot as an NHLer: size, speed, agility, vision, creativity, and even some bite.

Hamilton played one more full season of junior. While the NHL started 2012–13 in a lockout, Hamilton continued to prep in Niagara. He also played for Team Canada in the 2013 World Junior Championship. Once the lockout lifted, Hamilton reported to Boston and made the team as a 19-year-old. He did not look out of place. As a rookie, Hamilton scored five goals and 11 assists in 42 games. Hamilton and Seguin fell two wins short of winning the Cup.

That summer, as Seguin moved on to Dallas, Hamilton remained in Boston. He scored seven goals and 18 assists in 64 games in 2013–14, finding a home alongside Chara on the first pairing. As a third-year pro, Hamilton recorded 10 goals and 32 assists in 72 games. He led the team with 15 points on the power play. He averaged 21:20 of ice time per game, third-most after Chara and Dennis Seidenberg.

During exit meetings, Chiarelli and coach Claude Julien told Hamilton of their satisfaction with his development. Hamilton did not say anything unexpected.

But a month later, as new GM Don Sweeney spoke with J.P. Barry, Hamilton's agent, regarding an extension, Chiarelli's replacement learned something was wrong. Despite multiple offers, Hamilton declined to re-sign.

"We extended Dougie a very significant contract offer," Sweeney said. "It didn't lead us to where we thought he'd be comfortable being part of our group long term."

The Bruins were worried. The draft was approaching. If they were to trade Hamilton, the 2015 NHL Draft would be the best opportunity to replace a potential franchise defenseman. Prospects Noah Hanifin, Ivan Provorov, and Zach Werenski were highly touted defensemen.

The Bruins also didn't want to get to July 1, 2015, with Hamilton still in limbo. By that date, Hamilton was eligible to sign an offer sheet. Chiarelli, the Bruins' former GM, had resurfaced in Edmonton.

Chiarelli was sure to extend an offer sheet to Hamilton, either to land his former player or put the Bruins in a tight cap situation if they matched.

"We ran every scenario," said president Cam Neely. "Say the offer sheet is $49 million. Does it make sense for us to have another 7-times-7 player on the roster? And who knows what no-moves or no-trades are attached? If that's the case and we don't match, we get a first, second, and third. Now we don't have the player and we have to wait a year to get the assets."

So on June 26, 2015, the Bruins did what they never expected to do: trade Hamilton. In exchange for the defensemen, the Flames sent the Bruins a first-round pick and two second-rounders. Four days later, the Flames signed Hamilton to a six-year, $34.5 million extension.

"He's able to go back, retrieve pucks, exit the zone," said Calgary GM Brad Treliving. "His ability to deny entries. His ability to create offense both with his passing and his legs. His ability to get shots on net. We think this is a real good addition for us."

The Bruins once had Kessel as a foundation piece. They traded Kessel for two more. By June 26, 2015, all three had been moved.

44

CARRYING ON A TRADITION

Four games into life as NHLer, Milan Lucic recorded his first career Gordie Howe hat trick: goal, assist, fight.

Of the three accomplishments, Lucic, 19 years old at the time, was proudest of the scrap.

On October 12, 2007, at 12:46 of the first period, Lucic belted Los Angeles' Raitis Ivanans. The 6'4", 231-pound Ivanans didn't care for the hit. Ivanans, nine years older than Lucic, challenged the rookie. Lucic accepted. He held his own.

Lucic developed into something far more than a fighter. During eight seasons in Boston, Lucic became the NHL's premier power forward. In 566 games, Lucic scored 139 goals and 203 assists. The left wing's skating, once his biggest weakness, improved to the point where nobody dared to fill his lane when he accelerated to cruising speed. His hands were soft enough to make him a go-to top-six forward, usually paired with David Krejci. When the Bruins won the Stanley Cup in 2011, Lucic, Krejci, and Nathan Horton bulled over opponents with their brawn and racked up points with their skill.

But what turned Lucic into the Spoked-B come alive, much like predecessors Cam Neely and Terry O'Reilly, was his fighting spirit. Lucic first made a name for himself as an amateur player with his fists. His knuckles were what helped him gain NHL traction, first with his employer, then with the rest of the league.

Lucic was originally expecting to return to the Vancouver Giants, his junior team, in 2007–08. Instead, Lucic's pugnacity, energy, and fearlessness convinced his employers they could not afford to send him back to the Western Hockey League.

Lucic broke into the NHL wearing No. 62 and skating on the fourth line. It didn't take Lucic long to ascend to the first line in a No. 17 sweater, which became one of the most popular jerseys in New England. Bruins fans have always treasured players who are quick to drop their gloves. Lucic didn't mind shedding his mitts. In fact, he liked it. There was nobody he enjoyed fighting more than Mike Komisarek.

Komisarek was a stay-at-home right-side defenseman for Montreal during Lucic's rookie season. Because of their respective job descriptions, Komisarek and Lucic were often on the ice at the same time during Bruins-Canadiens games. Their collisions touched off earthquakes. So did their fights.

On November 13, 2008, with the Bruins leading the Canadiens by a 5–1 score, Komisarek charged Lucic. The two threw punches. Lucic landed more. By the end of the one-sided fight, Komisarek had injured his shoulder. Lucic was screaming, waving his arms, and encouraging his home fans to do the same.

Less than two weeks later, Komisarek was injured for the rematch at Bell Centre. Georges Laraque, Montreal's then-enforcer, had plans to knock Lucic out of uniform as well. During their first shift together, Laraque whacked Lucic on the leg with his stick. Laraque then asked Lucic to fight. The Bruin did not respond. As a top-liner skating with Marc Savard and Phil Kessel, Lucic was told by coach Claude Julien not to engage with Laraque, a regular healthy scratch.

"There was no way it was going to happen," Julien said of a Lucic-Laraque throwdown. "[Shawn] Thornton was there, ready for Georges. Nothing happened. My tough guy was ready for their tough guy. Simple as that. I told him not to fight. It was me."

Some of Lucic's punching bags may have wished Julien had issued similar instructions when they played the Bruins. Komisarek, Mark Bell, and Chris Neil were some of the hard-rock players Lucic turned to dust with his thunderous right hand.

But Lucic was just as dangerous throwing around his 6'3", 233-pound frame. On October 23, 2008, Lucic lined up Toronto's Mike Van Ryn. There were two victims: Van Ryn and the TD Garden glass. Just as Van Ryn let the puck loose up the right-side wall, Lucic approached from the defenseman's left and propelled him through the glass. An entire pane shattered upon the impact.

"It felt like an elephant hit me," Van Ryn told the *National Post*.

Lucic's NHL physicality came close to never blossoming. As a teenager, Lucic couldn't even make his Junior B team in Vancouver. At the time, scouts saw a slow, unskilled brute. Lucic almost quit hockey altogether.

He kept at it. As a 16-year-old, Lucic made the roster of the Delta Ice Hawks. He was soon promoted to the Junior A Coquitlam Express, where he recorded 23 points and 100 penalty minutes in 50 games in 2004–05.

The Giants, his hometown major junior team, caught notice. But first they asked Lucic to do something else. He was in attendance for a Giants game as a spectator. Somebody requested Lucic to wear a chicken suit and participate in an on-ice race during intermission. Lucic accepted. He would go on to do many more notable things on the Giants ice, including winning the Memorial Cup in 2006–07. He believed he would return to captain the Giants the following season. He was wrong.

In retrospect, the 19-year-old Lucic had no business playing junior hockey. He was already a man, despite the condition that

BEST DRAFT PICKS

In 2006, the Bruins picked Milan Lucic in the second round. It may not have even been their best selection of the bunch. Twenty-one slots after taking Lucic, the Bruins drafted Brad Marchand in the third round. The two left wings complemented the selection of Phil Kessel with the fifth overall pick. The bounty of three top-six forwards made 2006 one of the team's best drafts in history.

Other highlights: Patrice Bergeron (second round, 2003), P.J. Axelsson (seventh round, 1995), Ted Donato (fifth round, 1987), Don Sweeney (eighth round, 1984), Steve Kasper (fourth round, 1980), and Stan Jonathan (fifth round, 1975).

had taken inches off his height. By then, doctors had diagnosed Lucic with Scheuermann's Disease, which made the part of his back between the shoulders curve.

Some unfortunate opponents had teased Lucic about his condition on the ice. Lucic chased them down and beat them up. Nobody made the same mistake in the NHL. Had they tried, Lucic would not have pulled his punches.

The same hands that turned into gloves-off lethal weapons were just as good as putting pucks in nets. As a second-year NHLer, Lucic scored 17 goals and 25 assists, usually making his home on Savard's left flank. Savard (63 assists) was the line's disher. He often looked to Lucic as his first option.

A sprained ankle the next year limited Lucic to 50 games. But he came alive the following season, scoring 30 goals and 32 assists in 79 games. It was his most dominant season yet. He settled into his top-line role alongside Krejci and Horton. Lucic and Horton did the dirty work of mucking in the hazardous areas, bowling over opponents, and cleaning up the garbage. Krejci, the lightning to his wingers' thunder, used his skill and slipperiness to set up Lucic and Horton for scoring chances.

By the end of their playoff run, Horton had been knocked out by an Aaron Rome head shot. But Lucic helped power the Bruins to a Game 7 win over his hometown Canucks. The native of East Vancouver paraded around his home rink, the same arena in which he was drafted by the Bruins in 2006, with the Cup above his head. He loved every minute of it.

Lucic's Black-and-Gold career was not without controversy. On November 12, 2011, Buffalo goalie Ryan Miller left the Garden crease to play the puck. Lucic's eyes lit up. The left wing ramped up to high speed and sent the 175-pound Miller flying. Lucic did it because he could. None of the Sabres on the ice was equipped to take on Lucic.

Miller left the game early. But he stayed postgame to issue some pointed comments at Lucic.

"I just want to say what a piece of [expletive] I think Lucic is," Miller said. "Fifty pounds on me and he runs me like that. It's unbelievable. Everyone in this city sees him as a big, tough, solid player. I respected him for how hard he played. That was gutless. Gutless. Piece of [expletive]."

Lucic saved his heavy artillery for the hated Habs. Lucic and Komisarek clashed repeatedly. During the 2008–09 playoffs, Lucic was suspended for one game for cross-checking Montreal irritant Maxim Lapierre. On March 24, 2014, Lucic sticked Alexei Emelin below the belt. On October 16, 2014, Lucic made an obscene gesture at Canadiens fans as he headed toward the penalty box, which earned him a $5,000 fine.

Lucic capped his Bruins career with a second-round playoff exit against Montreal in 2014. The heavily favored Bruins could not do much against star goalie Carey Price. In the handshake line after

Game 7, Lucic threatened to kill Emelin and Dale Weise the following season.

"I'm not sorry that I did it," Lucic said. "I'm a guy that plays on emotion, and this is a game of emotions. Sometimes you make decisions out of emotion that might not be the best ones. That's what it is. I didn't make the NHL because I accepted losing or I accepted failure, and I think that's what's gotten me to this point and made me the player that I am."

Lucic never got the chance to follow through on his threat. On June 25, 2015, the Bruins traded the 27-year-old to Los Angeles for Colin Miller, Martin Jones, and a first-round pick. Lucic was entering the final season of his contract. The Bruins did not want to pay the price to extend the left wing. They were also disappointed with his 18-goal performance in 2014–15.

Black-and-Gold Lucic jerseys, however, are still popular at the Garden. For eight seasons, Lucic defined the role of power forward, not just in Boston but around the league. When prospect Lawson Crouse was asked to describe his game prior to the 2015 NHL Draft, Crouse compared himself to Lucic. In 566 career games as a Bruin, Lucic became not just a player but a position.

45

NIFTY

The Rangers had good intentions when they acquired Ken Hodge from the Bruins on May 26, 1976. Hodge was coming off a season in which he scored 25 goals and 36 assists. In New York, Hodge would be reunited with former running mate Phil Esposito. The reunion, the Rangers believed, would help them return to the playoffs, following a 29–42–9 finish. In Boston, the relationship between Hodge and coach Don Cherry was one that looked to be unsustainable.

"Things really started to go downhill when Cherry came to the club," Hodge told the *Boston Globe*. "He did all kinds of things to me, and I wasn't the only one put in that position. All kinds of things went wrong with the Bruins this season, but I'd rather not go into them."

Rangers general manager John Ferguson did not believe the trade would end up decidedly in the Bruins' favor.

Hodge lasted just one full season on Broadway. Rick Middleton, the player the Rangers sent north for Hodge's services, grew into one of the more skilled forwards of his generation. Of the 988 career

points Middleton scored over 14 seasons, 898 took place while wearing Black and Gold.

The Rangers saw the first stages of Middleton's potential. He had no trouble scoring 22 goals and 18 assists in 47 games as a rookie in 1974–75. But in New York, like he did during his junior career in Oshawa, Middleton didn't pay much attention to defense. His coaches never wanted him to. They were on him to score, which he did in bunches.

The Bruins had the pleasure of seeing Middleton's development through. In 1976–77, Middleton scored 20 goals and 22 assists in 72 games as a first-year Bruin. It did not take long for anybody to question why Middleton's nickname was Nifty. Middleton's hands were sublime. He saw plays happening before everybody else. Middleton blended his physical talent with a processing power that made him a shining offensive light on a team that desperately needed such touch.

Middleton landed on Causeway Street when the previous generation's star power was fading fast. Bobby Orr had bolted for Chicago. Esposito and Hodge were gone. Johnny Bucyk was entering the final segment of his career. The Big Bad Bruins from 1970 and 1972 were transitioning to the Lunchpail AC, a rougher, more blue-collar, and less talented version of its predecessor. As such, they were happy to take all the skill they could take.

It required, however, an unexpected connection between a player and coach of seemingly different minds. Middleton played a smooth, disciplined, cerebral style. Cherry wanted his charges to play anvil-and-hammer hockey. But even the hard-headed Cherry understood a creative talent like Middleton was a critical component on his roster. In turn, Middleton learned under Cherry that playing anything less than a 200-foot game would be cheating himself and his employers.

ON THIS DATE

MARCH 27, 1984

Rick Middleton records a goal and three assists in a 6–4 win over Quebec. Middleton reaches the 100-point threshold for the second time in his career.

By 1978–79, Middleton had bought in fully to Cherry's approach. As a fifth-year pro, Middleton led the Bruins in scoring with 38 goals and 48 assists in 71 games. Middleton was entering the most productive sector of his career. The season thudded to a crash, however, in the playoffs against Montreal. It was the year of too many men. As Middleton and his teammates expected, Harry Sinden gave Cherry his walking papers.

"He turned my career around," Middleton told the *Boston Globe* upon Cherry's dismissal. "He taught me the game, but not individually. He taught me in unison with everyone else on the team. He taught us to be a team. I ask myself, 'Why can't [Sinden and Cherry] work together?' But obviously they can't. It's a big loss to hockey and it's a bigger loss to Boston."

Cherry, while no longer on hand to watch over Middleton, had driven home his message regarding structure. In 1979–80, Middleton potted 40 goals, the first of five straight seasons he reached the threshold. The right wing helped to bridge the Bruins from the Lunchpail AC of Terry O'Reilly, Mike Milbury, and John Wensink to the teams of Ray Bourque. While the Bruins retained their identity of physical, no-nonsense players, Middleton was one of the exceptions—the scorer his teammates protected because his skill could not be replaced. The Bruins didn't have anybody else who could think the game and play as creatively as Middleton.

"I've seen them all, and Nifty's the best one-on-one player in hockey," Brad Park told *Sports Illustrated*. "Take anyone in the league, give Nifty the puck, and 90 percent of the time he'll turn the other guy inside out."

Middleton was at the height of his artistry when Barry Pederson was his center. In 1983–84, with Pederson doing the dishing (77 assists), Middleton buried 47 goals. Even after Pederson was dealt to Vancouver in the Cam Neely blockbuster, Middleton continued to produce.

Middleton's prowess nearly put the Bruins over the top in 1987–88. That year, which would be Middleton's last, the right wing scored 13 goals and 19 assists in 59 games. In the playoffs, Middleton scored five goals and five assists in 19 games. He was part of the team that made history in the second round by beating Montreal for the first time in the playoffs since 1945.

But after losing to Edmonton in the final, Middleton had closed out his career without a Cup. He did just about everything short of winning a championship. Middleton is the organization's fourth-leading scorer with 898 points, trailing only Bourque (1,506), Bucyk (1,339), and Esposito (1,012). His 402 goals and 496 assists make the most productive right wing in team history. That Middleton didn't make the Hockey Hall of Fame is a head scratcher.

"It had to be the scariest feeling in the world backing up and having Ricky come at you," Pederson said in *The Bruins: Brian McFarlane's Original Six*. "He never made the same move twice. So many of them were left grabbing at air."

46

A WELL-ROUNDED BOSS

ppropriately, Walter Brown will always be known as a basketball man. It is not just any executive who participates in the founding of the NBA, like Brown did in 1949. It is not just any business who founds the Boston Celtics, one of the NBA's most important franchises, in 1946. It is not just any owner who can call himself Bill Russell's boss. Under Brown's guidance, the Celtics became a dynasty. Appropriately, the Celtics retired No. 1 in Brown's honor in 1964.

Yet in 1962, three years before Brown was inducted into the Basketball Hall of Fame, the heralded hoops man was given his place of permanence in the Hockey Hall of Fame. Brown's contributions to the Bruins and to hockey were just as significant as those to the Celtics and to basketball.

Brown was a good hockey coach. Between 1930 and '40, Brown stood behind the bench of the Boston Olympics. Brown's teams won five national amateur championships. In 1933, the Olympics upset Team Canada in the World Championship, giving the Americans their first gold medal in the tournament's history. In 1950, when Brown was president of Boston Garden, he returned to coaching the Olympics temporarily after Freddie Metcalfe stepped away because of poor health.

Brown's reach expanded internationally. He served as chairman of the U.S. Olympic Ice Hockey Committee in 1960. Brown played a significant role in shaping the roster that would represent the country at Squaw Valley, California. Twenty years before the Miracle on Ice, the Americans, led by Massachusetts players such as Bill and Bob Cleary, won the country's first Olympic gold medal in hockey by rolling over Czechoslovakia in the final 9–4.

But Brown's most important achievement in Boston was giving the Bruins better financial security. He was in position to do as son of George Brown and steward of Boston Garden.

By the 1950s, the Bruins were not a healthy franchise. Owner Weston Adams, son of founder Charles Adams, was not happy with his club's financial direction. Adams fought the league's proposal to expand the season from 60 to 70 games, citing the sporting alternatives Bostonians could consider. The Olympics, formerly coached by Brown, were one of the Bruins' competitors.

"We have all kinds of school hockey and basketball and baseball all over our papers," Adams said in *Art Ross: The Hockey Legend Who Built the Bruins*. "We have more competition in Boston than any other city in the league."

Two other factors played parts in the Bruins' misfortunes. Television, Adams believed, discouraged fans from attending games at the Garden. They did not have much incentive to pay for games in person when they could watch for free at home. The Bruins also had a landlord. They did not own the Garden. Brown and his colleagues at Boston Garden Arena Corporation did. There were always rumors that Brown and the Garden were interested in purchasing the team. They were about to come true.

In 1950–51, the Bruins went 22–30–18. Milt Schmidt scored 22 goals and 39 assists in 62 games to win the Hart Trophy as the league MVP. Schmidt and Bill Quackenbush (5–24–29 in 70 games) were named First Team All-Stars. But the Garden was not a kind home. The Bruins went a mediocre 13–12–10 on Causeway Street.

The Bruins would have selected goalie Tuukka Rask with their No. 22 pick in 2005 had Toronto not done so at No. 21. But a year later, Boston acquired Rask from Toronto in exchange for veteran goaltender Andrew Raycroft. It's easy to see who won that trade.

Even worse, the Bruins lost $80,000 that season. It got so bad that in the fall of 1951, Adams declined to pay for the team's training camp. This could not continue.

On October 11, 1951, Brown and the Garden Corporation purchased a majority stake of the Bruins from Adams. According to the *Boston Globe*, the sale price for 60 percent of the organization was $179,520. Brown became team president, succeeding Adams. Brown became one of the busiest executives in pro sports as the man in charge of both the Bruins and the Celtics.

The Bruins did not improve in their first season under new ownership. In 1951–52, the Bruins went 25–29–16. One of the season's highlights was Bobby Bauer coming out of retirement on March 18, 1952, to play one final game with Kraut Line mates Woody Dumart and Milt Schmidt. Even if the team's on-ice fortunes did not turn around immediately, Brown liked the club's direction. He approved of the leadership of coach Lynn Patrick. Brown classified Art Ross as the best candidate as general manager. Schmidt was the best competitor Brown ever saw.

"No professional sports team ever put out any more than these Bruins," Brown told the *Boston Globe* at year's end. "I want to thank them collectively for what they have done to restore interest in the sport."

The Bruins rewarded Brown for his faith in the team. The next year, the Bruins returned to the Stanley Cup Final, where they lost four of five games to the Canadiens. For the rest of the decade, the Bruins could not crack the dominance of the Canadiens and Red Wings, the NHL's two strongest teams.

The Bruins hit the skids at the start of the 1960s, missing the playoffs in eight straight seasons. Brown died in 1964, after which Adams repurchased the Bruins from the Garden Corporation.

Brown's legacy would live on following his death. In 1971, Boston University opened Walter Brown Arena. Every year, the Gridiron Club of Greater Boston names a winner for the Walter Brown Award. Walter Brown Arena is still open for hockey. The Walter Brown Award is given to the best American-born New England player competing in college hockey. The man more associated with basketball made his mark on hockey.

47

STEALING AN ACE

I n 2005, the Bruins pegged Tuukka Rask as one of the five top picks in the draft. That season, they would not pick until No. 22, well past the time they projected Rask to be gone.

Rask was still around when the Maple Leafs approached the podium to make their pick at No. 21. You can imagine the disappointment at the Bruins table when Toronto picked Rask at No. 21, making him the second goalie to go in the draft after Carey Price (Montreal, fifth overall).

A year later, the Bruins had another chance at Rask. The Leafs were looking for an experienced goalie. The Bruins had one in Andrew Raycroft, who won the Calder Trophy as the league's best rookie in 2003–04. In 2006, Raycroft was 26 years old, in the sweet spot for NHL goalies. But he was coming off a down season in which he went 8–19–2 with a 3.71 goals-against average and an .879 save percentage. Raycroft wanted out. The Bruins honored his request.

The Bruins chose to sell low with Raycroft. But they never imagined their return would be as high as Rask. In 2005–06, the former Leafs prospect went 12–7–8 with a 2.09 GAA and a .926 save percentage for Ilves Tampere of the Finnish SM-Liiga. As an 18-year-old that season, Rask was playing with and against men. He proved he was no boy.

Despite Rask's first-round pedigree and his potential, the Leafs decided he would be the one to go for Raycroft. They had another puck-stopping prospect in Justin Pogge, their third-round pick in 2004. On June 24, 2006, on the first day of the 2006 NHL Draft, interim general manager Jeff Gorton acquired Rask for Raycroft.

"I'll tell you, though, this kid is the real deal," Bill Zito, Rask's agent, told the *Boston Globe*. "He spent half of last season with Ilves. That's the men's league, not kids, and he played on the Finnish national team, too. Great kid, and an unbelievable prospect."

Rask proved Zito's words to be true. Rask has become the Bruins' ace and one of the best goalies in the NHL. He is smooth in the net, technical at all times, under control, and explosive and athletic when he needs to make a bail-out save. The same could not be said for the goalie who went the other way.

Raycroft became Toronto's No. 1 goalie. In 2006–07, Raycroft appeared in 72 games, going 37–25–9 with a 2.99 GAA and an .894 save percentage. But he lasted just one more season in Toronto. In 2007–08, Raycroft lost the starting job to Vesa Toskala. He played three more NHL seasons as a backup in Vancouver, Dallas, and Colorado. Raycroft never matched his performance from his rookie year.

Pogge, the prospect the Leafs kept instead of Rask, played in only seven games for the Leafs. On August 10, 2009, Toronto traded Pogge to Anaheim for a sixth-round pick in 2011. Less than a year later, the Ducks moved Pogge and a fourth-round pick to Carolina for Aaron Ward. He made subsequent professional stops in Sweden and Italy.

Meanwhile, Rask's precocious play in Finland served to be a good indicator of his future success in North America. Following the trade, Rask played one more season for Ilves, going 18–18–10 with a 2.38 GAA and a .926 save percentage. He arrived in Boston as a 20-year-old in the fall of 2007, and promptly outperformed Tim Thomas and Manny Fernandez in training camp. But the Bruins knew that starting Rask with the varsity would not be good for his development. Rask wasn't happy with his demotion to Providence. But it was where he had to be to launch his North American career.

In the AHL, Rask quickly learned the smaller rinks changed the way he had to play. Pucks were on him quicker. So were angry forwards. The AHL was a hostile and boisterous environment for the laid-back Finn. Some of it rubbed off.

On March 20, 2009, during his second season in Providence, Rask was in goal for a shootout against the Albany River Rats. Two goals went in. Rask didn't believe either should have counted. After the second, a shot by Harrison Reed that clanged off the bottom of the crossbar and into the net, referee Frederick L'Ecuyer called it a good goal. Rask smacked his stick on the crossbar in disagreement. Then as he skated off the ice, Rask smashed his stick into the boards, then flung it back onto the ice. Once he retreated into the tunnel, Rask spotted a milk crate. That went flying onto the ice too.

"Right over the top of my head," said former teammate Johnny Boychuk, who was also in Providence at the time. "If I was about 5 to 10 feet further ahead, it probably would have hit me. Hey, I was mad, too. Everybody was mad. It just so happened to be a milk crate going by. Tossed it like Joe Montana."

Rask was tagged with a game misconduct. He was not suspended. His boss didn't mind the penalty.

Part of the reason the Bruins wanted Rask to develop in Providence was to build up his mental game. Rask is naturally calm. He had to learn how to compete.

"I told him not to do it again," said GM Peter Chiarelli. "But I said, 'That's the type of fire you don't have to show overtly, but that's the type of fire I want in players and goalies.' Tuukka has a calm demeanor about him, in contrast to Tim [Thomas]. They're both competitive, but Tim's got more battle. But a fire burns in Tuukka. We've seen that. That's one example of it."

Rask left Providence behind for good in 2009–10. Rask went 22–12–5 with a 1.97 GAA and a .931 save percentage, the latter two statistics being good enough to lead the league. With Thomas not at 100 percent because of an injured hip, Rask nabbed the starting job and took it into the playoffs. Rask backstopped the Bruins to a first-round win over Buffalo. But he was in net for the team's second-round collapse against Philadelphia when the Flyers rallied from an 0–3 deficit to advance to the Eastern Conference Final.

Rask ceded the starting job back to Thomas for the next two years. But once Thomas declared his decision to step away from hockey for one year following the 2011–12 season, Rask became the ace. He has yet to give away the title. In 2012–13, Rask almost helped to deliver the second Cup in three seasons to the Bruins. A year later, Rask went 36–15–6 with a 2.04 GAA and a .930 save percentage to win the Vezina Trophy as the league's best goalie, beating out Colorado's Semyon Varlamov and Tampa Bay's Ben Bishop.

On June 27, 2014, the Bruins hired John Ferguson as executive director of player personnel. Eight years earlier, Ferguson was the GM in Toronto when the Leafs traded Rask for Raycroft. It was a decision that contributed to Ferguson's firing on January 22, 2008. Ferguson was happy to be reunited with the goalie he once traded away. It's a good thing to consider Rask a teammate.

48

ALL TINY, ALL THE' TIME

On September 28, 1929, the NHL passed a groundbreaking rule. From then on, players would be eligible to pass the puck forward to a teammate. It was a revolutionary but necessary change in the offense-throttled league. Tiny Thompson was partly responsible for instituting one of the most important rule changes in NHL history.

The year before, the Bruins won their first Stanley Cup. In three games against Montreal in the semifinal, Thompson allowed just two goals. While the Bruins scored four goals in two wins over the Rangers to win the Cup, Thompson let just one puck slip behind him during the two-game series. Thompson was too good at his job.

The Bruins had acquired Thompson from the Minneapolis Millers of the American Hockey Association ahead of the 1928–29 season. General manager Art Ross believed Thompson could contend with Hal Winkler for the goaltending job. Ross was right. Winkler, who had been the Bruins' primary puck stopper the two previous seasons, never played in Boston again. Thompson won the job, even

though the rookie had never seen a minute of NHL action. It would be Thompson's crease for a long time.

During the NHL's first years, it was common for teams to go with one goalie for long stretches. But Thompson's run was special. He played every game of his rookie season. He was the Bruins' only goalie in 1929–30. Thompson went 44 straight against in 1930–31. It wasn't until January 16, 1932, that an injured Thompson finally ceded the crease. Percy Jackson replaced Thompson in goal for a 2–2 road tie against the Canadiens. Thompson had played in 154 straight games. Ten days later at home, after playing the first period against the Maroons, Thompson gave up the net to Jackson. It was the first time any goalie other than Thompson had visited Boston Garden's home crease.

Thompson deserved every start. Even after the rule change allowing the forward pass was instituted, Thompson remained reliable amid the offensive assault. In 1929–30, the first season following the amended rule, Thompson backstopped the Bruins to a 38–5–1 record. The team's .837 winning percentage remains the best of any team in NHL history. Thompson posted a 2.19 goals-against average, allowing just 98 pucks to end up in his net. Naturally, Thompson won the Vezina Trophy as the league's top ace. It was the first of four times Thompson would win the Vezina. Thompson and the Bruins were upset, however, by Montreal in the final.

Thompson was used to being a perpetual inhabitant of the Boston net. But in 1930–31, Thompson made news by leaving it. In the playoffs, the Bruins lost to the Canadiens in the semifinal, three games to two. The premature end of the season wasn't what would be remembered.

In Game 2 of the series, the Bruins trailed by one goal in the third period. They were shorthanded because George Owen was in the penalty box. Ross, from his position behind the bench, did

ON THIS DATE

FEBRUARY 21, 1933

Tiny Thompson stops all 23 shots he sees against the Canadiens. There is no need for such perfection, as his teammates light up the Canadiens 10-0. It is the most goals scored by one team that season.

not like his chances of tying the game with one man down. So Ross instructed Thompson to come off the ice, replacing his goalie with an extra skater in Art Chapman. League historians believe it was the first time a coach had pulled his goalie and left his net open for an extra attacker.

Two years later, the Bruins asked Thompson to remain in his net for one of the league's most historic nights. The Bruins and Maple Leafs squared off in the semifinal. The teams split the first four games, setting up a do-or-die Game 5 at Maple Leafs Gardens on April 3, 1933. Neither team intended to go home early. Thompson and Toronto counterpart Lorne Chabot stopped every puck they saw through regulation. Their puck-stopping prowess continued for much longer.

After more than 100 minutes of scoreless play, Ross and Toronto GM Conn Smythe petitioned NHL president Frank Calder to halt the game and continue it the next day. Calder denied their request. It wasn't until the sixth overtime that a puck finally hit the back of a net.

Eddie Shore tried to make a pass up the ice. Andy Blair intercepted Shore's pass and spotted Ken Doraty going to the net. After receiving Blair's pass, Doraty made no mistake, tucking the puck behind Thompson after 164:46 of play. It was the longest game ever played in the NHL. Thompson faced 112 shots, also a league record. Upon conclusion of the season, Thompson claimed his second Vezina Trophy.

In 1935–36, Thompson won his third Vezina. That season, he also became the first goalie to record an assist. His time in Boston would expire in 1938 after getting hurt in an intrasquad game. A puck off the stick of Bobby Bauer open a cut over Thompson's right eye, a wound that required five stitches to close. Thompson's injury gave Frank Brimsek his opportunity. Brimsek took advantage of his chance, forcing the Bruins to wheel Thompson to Detroit on November 28. 1938.

"I'm sorry, of course, to leave Boston, where I have many friends and where the fans have always treated me well," Thompson told the *Boston Globe*. "But, in other ways, I'm glad to get away and I think I'll get along fine with Jack Adams and the Red Wings."

The trade worked in the Bruins' favor. The unknown Brimsek turned into "Mr. Zero" after posting six shutouts in his first seven games. The Wings went 18–24–6 with Thompson serving as their No. 1 goalie. Thompson played one more season with Detroit before retiring. He was inducted into the Hockey Hall of Fame in 1959.

BENCH BECOMES HIS BEAT

n October of 2000, following a 3–4–1 start, general manager Harry Sinden fired Pat Burns. Following his sacking, the coach did not hold a press conference at the FleetCenter, where most of such business is conducted. Instead, Burns addressed his firing at the Christmas Island Steakhouse and North Pole Tavern in Laconia, New Hampshire, one of the haunts he and his motorcycle-riding friends preferred.

That was just the kind of guy Burns was: a maverick.

"Life's too short to point fingers and have vengeance against people, to be bitter," Burns told the *Boston Globe* after his dismissal. "Life is too short for that, so move on and let's go. I think the decision that was made was a business decision. I felt Harry didn't want to do it. He felt he had to do it, and he said, 'I don't know if it's the right one or the wrong one, I'm ready to live with it.' I don't know if it's the right one or the wrong one, either, but I have to live with it. I have no bad feelings toward anyone in that organization. Life goes on. I'm just a simple guy trying to get through life. This is a bump that I happened to hit along the way and I'll recover from it. I hope and pray for them, that they do well. I still have a part of me in that hockey club."

Burns' firing ended a run that did not last very long. On May 21, 1997, after originally considering Boston University coach Jack Parker, Sinden hired Burns as Steve Kasper's replacement. Burns lasted until October 25, 2000, when he was replaced by Mike Keenan. But in those three-plus seasons of work behind the Bruins' bench, Burns helped to revitalize a franchise that was in desperate need of a caffeine fix.

The Bruins hired Burns to give the team structure and credibility after Kasper, who had famously benched Cam Neely and Kevin Stevens, was shown the door. In Burns, Sinden landed a coach who had twice been considered the best in the business: first in 1989 with Montreal, then again in 1993 with Toronto. It did not take Burns long to turn the trick a third time.

The Bruins needed immediate help. The organization's streak of 29 straight seasons with a postseason appearance had come to an end. They had staggered to a 26–47–9 record, worst in the league. There was no better choice than Burns to lead the turnaround.

Burns was not much of a player. But he knew two things well: accountability and coaching. For the former, Burns' training ground as a policeman in Gatineau, Quebec, came in handy. For the latter, Burns succeeded at every stop prior to Boston: in juniors with the Hull Olympiques, then in the NHL with the Canadiens and Maple Leafs.

Burns had two tasks upon his arrival in Boston. First, he had to lead the Bruins back to respectability. A second straight playoff no-show would not be acceptable. For that, Burns leaned on his two most important players: captain Ray Bourque (13 goals, 35 assists) and goalie Byron Dafoe (30–25–9, 2.24 goals-against average, .914 save percentage). The two stalwarts led the Bruins to a 39–30–13 record, good enough to get the team back into the playoffs, although they lost to the Capitals in the opening round. They had help from up-and-coming No. 1 center Jason Allison and a stout checking line P.J. Axelsson, Tim Taylor, and Rob DiMaio.

These components helped deliver a third Jack Adams Award into Burns' trophy case. Burns remains the only coach to win the award three times in his first seasons with his new clubs. It is a testament to the turnaround touch Burns had mastered.

Burns' second chore was a long-term assignment. Before Burns had ever stepped behind the Boston bench, he claimed a prized possession: a future franchise center. In June of 1997, the Bruins selected 18-year-old Joe Thornton with the No. 1 pick. There was no debate about how good Thornton would become. The 6'4" left-shot center had every tool a coach would want. Thornton could protect the puck. He could dish and shoot. He could create plays out of nothing. He had a frame that would not break down, regardless of the punishment NHL opponents were sure to deliver.

In some ways, given Thornton's projection, grooming him into a superstar was the more important mission for Burns. It would be the coach's responsibility to ease Thornton into the league at the right pace to ensure his future success. Burns made sure to see the plan through.

That year, Burns unleashed fellow teenager Sergei Samsonov on the league. The skilled right wing, selected seven slots after Thornton, tore up the NHL for 22 goals and 25 assists in 81 games. Samsonov won the Calder Trophy as the league's ace rookie. Burns had no intention of letting Thornton play with similar freedom.

Samsonov regularly played on Burns' first line with Dmitri Khristich and Jason Allison. He afforded no such luxury to Thornton. The first overall pick spent most of his rookie season parked on the fourth line—that is, when he played at all. In 55 games, Thornton scored just three goals and four assists. Usually, the fourth line is not a home for skilled and powerful pivots. But Burns correctly identified that Thornton was not ready for heavier lifting. Had Burns given Thornton more rope, the rookie would not have survived the rigors of the NHL. Burns preached slow and steady with Thornton.

While the teenager might not have agreed with his boss' approach, it turned out to be right in the long run. Thornton played 81 games in each of the next two seasons. In 1999–2000, Burns' last full season in Boston, Thornton led the team in scoring with 23 goals and 37 assists for 60 points. But Thornton didn't have enough help. The Bruins missed the playoffs for the second time in four seasons. After the Bruins stumbled at the start of the following season, Sinden had seen enough.

The Stanley Cup that eluded Burns in Boston, Montreal, and Toronto finally became his in New Jersey in 2003. A year later, Burns was diagnosed with colon cancer. Five years later, the disease returned, this time in his lungs. In March of 2010, Burns attended a groundbreaking ceremony at Stanstead College for a rink built in his name.

"I probably won't see the project to the end, but let's hope I'm looking down on it and see a young Wayne Gretzky or Mario Lemieux," Burns said in his speech. "I know my life is nearing its end and I accept that. As for my career, I always said to my kids, 'You don't cry because it's over, you're happy because it happened.' That's the main thing. I'm happy it happened."

Burns died on November 9, 2010. He was elected to the Hockey Hall of Fame in 2014.

50

A SECOND CUP IS LOST

With just two more wins, the Bruins could have started talk of a dynasty. In 2013, two years after claiming their first Stanley Cup since 1972, the Bruins were right back on the edge of swiping a second trophy.

Their path to a second championship, however, took a double-barreled pounding in Game 5 of the final against Chicago. The Blackhawks won at United Center 3–1 to take a 3–2 series lead. The Bruins suffered another setback during the loss—the departure of their best all-around player.

During the series, Bergeron absorbed damage that was more fitting of a car crash. In Game 4, Bergeron took a wicked thump from Michael Frolik, one that left him with torn rib cartilage. In Game 5, Bergeron was subject to the typical pounding of the playoffs. This time, it was bad enough to knock him out of the game. In the first period, Bergeron took a big hit on his left side. For two periods, Bergeron played through a broken rib. But during second intermission, Bergeron was taken to a nearby Chicago hospital. His status for Game 6 was in doubt.

The Bruins were a good team in 2012–13. Upon the end of the lockout, the players that had fled to Europe for playing time—Bergeron played for Lugano in Switzerland's National League A—swarmed back to North America for 48 games of fast and furious postseason prep work.

Tim Thomas was serving his one-year absence away from hockey, citing fatigue and a need to reconnect with his family. But Tuukka Rask was ready to claim the starting job. Other than Thomas, most of the 2011 Cup-winning band was back and hungry after their first-round exit to Washington the year before. Tyler Seguin had replaced Mark Recchi alongside Bergeron and Brad Marchand. David Krejci was centering Milan Lucic and Nathan Horton. Dougie Hamilton, the team's first-round pick in 2011, was adjusting to his first pro season.

Prior to the trade deadline, the Bruins sent a conditional first-round pick and two mid-level prospects to Dallas for Jaromir Jagr. The ageless Jagr, 41 at the time, replaced Seguin on Bergeron's right side.

The Bruins nearly flamed out against Toronto in the first round. But their third-period rally in Game 7 and overtime victory injected them with much-needed energy and confidence to roll through their two following opponents. They needed just five games to roll through the Rangers in the second round to set up an Eastern Conference Final showdown against the powerful Penguins.

Pittsburgh had plenty of weapons. Sidney Crosby and Evgeni Malkin were the most lethal 1–2 center combination in the league. While Marc-Andre Fleury didn't have good postseason results, he was sharp enough to steal games. And the Penguins had acquired late-season help from Calgary in Jarome Iginla—who was, at least to then-GM Peter Chiarelli's mind, a temporary Bruin.

Jagr, acquired on April 2, was not the Bruins' original target. Iginla, the longtime Calgary captain, was in their crosshairs. The Flames, under then-GM Jay Feaster, were rebuilding. Iginla's contract was expiring, and the right wing did not intend to re-sign with the only club he considered his employer. Iginla was Calgary's best trade chip. The Bruins went all in.

On March 27, the Bruins thought they had won their prize. Chiarelli agreed to send Matt Bartkowski, Alexander Khokhlachev, and a first-round pick to the Flames for Iginla. Khokhlachev, then playing for Providence of the AHL, was scratched from that night's game against Portland. Bartkowski would not play that night against Montreal. The Bruins promoted Torey Krug from Providence to replace Bartkowski. The Flames planned to sit Iginla against Colorado. But Iginla had other ideas.

Iginla knew that Pittsburgh, the top team in the Eastern Conference, represented his best shot at winning the Cup, a trophy he had never lifted. He was a linemate with Crosby during the 2010 Olympics. Iginla had a no-trade clause. He exercised it, even after Feaster and Chiarelli had agreed upon the deal. Iginla wanted to go to Pittsburgh.

So the trade that had seemingly been made was starting to be unmade. Chiarelli was met with radio silence whenever he tried to contact Feaster later that day. Chiarelli started to worry that something had gone off the rails. He was right. The Penguins landed Iginla from Calgary for a first-round pick and Ken Agostino and Ben Hanowski, two college prospects. Pittsburgh's package was not as good as Boston's.

"These things happen all the time, more than you know, about deals going south for whatever reason," Chiarelli said after Iginla slipped through his fingers. "We believed we had a deal. We operated on the premise of a deal. When things were silent—in my experience, you know when things go silent, usually something is going screwy from your end. And it was."

By the third round, Iginla had settled on Malkin's left wing. The Penguins were favored to beat the Bruins and advance to the final. The series was over before the Penguins knew what hit them. The Bruins ran Iginla and the Penguins out of the playoffs in four straight

ON THIS DATE
JUNE 7, 2013

Tuukka Rask stops all 26 shots in the Bruins' 1–0 win over Pittsburgh in Game 4 of the Eastern Conference Final to complete the sweep. The Bruins allow just two goals total, tying a team record for fewest allowed in a four-game series.

games. The Bruins had the last laugh on Iginla, who would sign with the team the following season.

The Bruins' fourth and final opponent was Chicago. The Blackhawks were the Ferrari to the Bruins' Ford F-150. Fast, quick, and skilled players such as Jonathan Toews, Patrick Kane, Patrick Sharp, and Duncan Keith paced Chicago's go-go attack. Pucks did not stray long in Chicago's defensive zone before they landed on forwards' sticks up the ice.

Despite Chicago's advantage in skill, the Bruins were close to setting up Game 7 in Chicago. The Blackhawks, down 2–1 in the third period, pulled Corey Crawford for an extra attacker. With 1:16 remaining in regulation, Bryan Bickell beat Tuukka Rask to tie Game 6 2–2. Seventeen seconds later, after gaining net-front position on Johnny Boychuk, Dave Bolland tipped Johnny Oduya's shot past Rask for the winning goal.

Shortly after the loss, Bergeron went to nearby Massachusetts General Hospital because he had trouble breathing. Doctors learned the extent of his injuries: punctured lung, broken rib, separated shoulder. It took two days before Bergeron was well enough to leave the hospital. The savagery of the playoffs had punished one of the Bruins' best players. The suddenness of the exit might have been just as painful.